In a culture that offers endless opportunities to hone our skills and our knowledge, Zack Eswine invites us to hone our wisdom. Growing in wisdom often feels inconvenient and unimportant, but leaving this area underdeveloped has wrecked countless lives. And personally, I don't want to be one of them. For that reason, I'm deeply thankful for *Wiser with Jesus* and its timely warning not to forsake the cultivation of wisdom. I closed this book feeling deeply loved, expertly counseled, and filled with hope.

KELLY NEEDHAM
Wife and mom of five; author, *Purposefooled*

I have long appreciated Zack's thoughtful pastoral wisdom. What a delight to see him apply this through the biblical theme of wisdom, inviting us to humbly and imperfectly find in Jesus the wisdom we need for our complex lives.

JONATHAN T. PENNINGTON
Professor of New Testament, Southern Baptist Theological Seminary, Louisville, Kentucky;
author, *Jesus the Great Philosopher*

Reading *Wiser with Jesus* feels very much like having a chat in a busy cafe with the author. And that's great! Zack is a congenial guy and good company, he always listens carefully, and he gently helps us discern what is true and wise amid the noise and chatter around us. So this is clearly a book for 'such a time as this'. In a culture that idolises the new and the strong, the Bible's ancient voice of wisdom gets drowned out or ignored. What's needed is for some in our generation to plumb its depths and then translate afresh the better way in the old, old story, and this Zack has achieved superbly.

MARK MEYNELL
Director (Europe and Caribbean)

Steve Jobs said: "I would trade all of my technology for an afternoon with Socrates". *Wiser with Jesus* is an invitation to trade all of your folly for an afternoon with Jesus – through the accessible, deep, poetic and graceful language of Zack Eswine. Zack has been wounded, yet in God's healing process he found light into the cracks. In the journey of becoming whole, this transformation refined him into a trusted guide to wisdom. As you enter this book, humbly acknowledge your own wisdom deficit: in the age of information, we are unaware we have lost true knowledge and wise living. We have become seduced by lesser metals and content with unrefined ore. Yet, amidst metals of lesser value, Eswine is offering you previously unknown mining tools that will potentially refine you into a golden heart.

DAVI C. RIBEIRO LIN
Assistant Professor of Pastoral Theology and Ministry,
Gordon-Conwell Theological Seminary

In all honesty I wish this book was written twenty years ago when I started out in pastoral ministry. In *Wiser with Jesus*, Zack Eswine offers pastors and ministry leaders a profound and deeply human guide to embodying Christ-like wisdom within the demands of pastoral care. With humility and a refreshing honesty, Eswine carefully unpacks the wisdom literature, guiding us as to how it speaks into the specific, often messy, realities of today's ministry contexts. My prayer is that this book will increasingly become a vital companion for those committed to faithfully stewarding the precious lives entrusted to their care.

DAN STEEL
Principal, Yarnton Manor, Oxford

Zack has given us a true treasure—poetic yet practical, bold yet compassionate. Rooted in the ancient wisdom of Scripture and beautifully original, this book will draw you closer to Jesus and lead you into a life of wholeness and joy.

Ken Shigematsu
Pastor, Tenth Church, Vancouver, British Columbia;
author, God in My Everything

Zack Eswine is the sage our modern church culture needs. He will deny it, but that will prove the point. Wisdom seeps out of every pore of this book. But it is not the sort of wisdom that fits well in 140 characters and is pithy but shallow. It is the sort of wisdom that comes from a deep and abiding relationship with his savior. Patient, kind, long-suffering, joyful, humble wisdom. In this book, Lady Wisdom cries out, "Whoever is simple, let him turn in here!" And the humble, looking for wisdom, will respond.

Elyse Fitzpatrick
Author and speaker

Zack Eswine

WISER
with
JESUS

Overcoming the Temptations that Hinder Your
Relationships, Steal Your Time, Mar Your
Decision-Making and Thwart Your Purpose

FOCUS

Unless otherwise stated the Scripture quotations are from The Holy Bible, English Standard Version, copyright © 2001 by Crossway Bibles, a publishing ministry of Good News Publishers. Used by permission. All rights reserved.

Scripture quotations marked 'NIV' are from The Holy Bible, New International Version, Copyright © 1973, 1978, 1984, 2011 by Biblica, Inc.™ Used by permission. All rights reserved worldwide.

Scripture quotations marked CSB have been taken from the Christian Standard Bible®, Copyright © 2017 by Holman Bible Publishers. Used by permission. Christian Standard Bible® and CSB® are federally registered trademarks of Holman Bible Publishers.

Scripture quotations marked (NLT) are taken from the Holy Bible, New Living Translation, copyright © 1996. Used by permission of Tyndale House Publishers, Inc., Wheaton, Illinois 60189. All rights reserved.

Copyright © Zack Eswine 2025

paperback ISBN 978-1-5271-1223-0
ebook ISBN 978-1-5271-1288-9

10 9 8 7 6 5 4 3 2 1

Published in 2025

by

Christian Focus Publications Ltd.,
Geanies House, Fearn, Ross-shire
IV20 1TW, Great Britain.

www.christianfocus.com

Cover design by Jess Fadel

Printed and bound by
Bell and Bain Glasgow

All rights reserved. No part of this publication may be reproduced, stored in a retrieval system, or transmitted, in any form, by any means, electronic, mechanical, photocopying, recording or otherwise without the prior permission of the publisher or a licence permitting restricted copying. In the U.K. such licences are issued by the Copyright Licensing Agency, 4 Battlebridge Lane, London, SE1 2HX www.cla.co.uk

For Jessica

Contents

Acknowledgements — 11
Introduction — 13

Part One: *Relationally* Wiser with Jesus

1. Your Wisdom Story and Mine — 23
2. When We're Naive — 37
3. When We're Foolish — 51
4. When We Scoff — 67
5. When We're Crushed in Spirit — 83
6. The Menu of Loves — 99

Part Two: *Skillfully* Wiser with Jesus

7. Making Better Decisions — 117
8. Anchoring Your Life in God's Steadfast Love — 135
9. Getting a Better Handle on Time — 151
10. Your Youth, Gray Hairs, and Old Age — 167
11. Postscript — 183

Endnotes — 185

Acknowledgements

I want to thank the Riverside congregation for the gift of doing life together—particularly the elders and leaders who remind me of hope, encourage me in my gifts, bear with me and invite me to trust Jesus amid my faults. I especially thank the vibrant community of counselors and mental health caregivers at Riverside, many of whom read an early draft of Part 1 of this book and whose advice helps me, not only as a writer, but as a pastor and friend. Thanks especially to Jennifer Morgan, Joel Chappaeu, Susan Greenplate, Devin Feeney, Tracie Wallace, Brian Masat, Lianne Johnson, and Lilian & Brad Werner.

I'd also like to thank Katy Martin, Joe Choi, and Mark Ryan for their invaluable counsel, partnership, and encouragement. Additional thanks are due to Dave DeWit, whose counsel and encouragement helped me at a low moment when it seemed this book might not come to be. Thanks also to Riverside's morning men's study, including Matt Fagin, Bob Holmes, and Gary Leibovich, who gave helpful feedback on an early draft.

Thanks, too, to our early sage leader's test cohorts in which this content was first introduced. Thanks especially to Doug Hon, Melissa Mckinney, Cole Lescher, Ben Loos, Jamin Roller, Andrew Seeley, Rick Whitlock, Bruwer Vroon, Lee Ruppel, and Clive Parnell, who offered timely and ongoing feedback and suggestions.

I'm grateful to Willie Mackenzie, Colin Fast and the team at Christian Focus, who encouraged me as a writer and enabled a book like this to be published. Special thanks to Helen Jones who served as my editor.

And, most of all, to Jessica, whose editing and suggestions in early drafts helped me grow and become clearer as a writer. Her steadfast encouragement helped me keep going when I felt too time-eaten, naive, foolish, and broken apart to write a book like this. Grace upon grace.

Introduction

*The path I walk
Christ walks it.[1]*

Once, I was stuck midway on a snowy mountain with no way out but down. I was a novice at skiing. I found myself stuck on a slope too advanced for my skill.

My friend Bob committed to traveling with me. He modeled the posture I needed and taught me the pace the mountain required. "Bend your knees and crouch forward, and Zachary," he said, "Embrace the speed."

Embracing the speed meant accepting that a safe arrival down this mountain would require a pace different than I wanted. After multiple tumbles, I finally slalomed down to solid ground.

Growing wiser with Jesus depends upon a similar trio of graces. To find wisdom's solid ground means learning to rely upon "a person, a posture, and a pace."[2]

Wisdom is a Person

Counsel in a person's heart is deep water;
but *a person of understanding* draws it out (Prov. 20:5 CSB).

All of us search and scroll for "a person of understanding" to make sense of our lives. Notice who you quote or don't, who you read and watch or won't, and who you're following to provide understanding will grow more apparent to you.

According to the wise, it's right and good to pause and ask, "Who will guide us?" (Matt. 15:14). But we need a guide who is no hack, someone who has expertise in handling the real life conditions and purposes that confront us. Someone who's been there and knows how to get through to the other side and thrive.

Jesus teaches this need for wise guidance by describing a blind man who knows he needs guidance. But if the blind man chooses someone equally unable to see, the trusted guide will not possess the ability to get them safely home. Both will get hurt (Matt. 15:14).

This book seeks to help you better discern the difference between persons of understanding and likable but mistaken or deceptive guides. Such a person:

- Recognizes and relishes any sighting of wisdom in your life (Prov. 10:23).
- Resists belittling you and your people (Prov. 11:12).
- Easily and expertly locates the wisdom that eludes you and kindly helps you see it (Prov. 14:6).
- Listens to your murky deep-water soul as their soul is at rest (Prov. 14:33).
- Discerns and gently exposes your unwise joys (Prov. 15:21).
- Is teachable and humble with you (Prov. 17:10; 19:25).
- Keeps a cool head, will not spew words at you (Prov. 17:27).

- Is better than being coached by an entire group of wanna-be-leaders (Prov. 28:2).

Did you notice in this list how a person of understanding is known by the way he relates to you? In contrast to Western Philosophy, which prioritizes content, Old Testament sages taught their students to approach wisdom not as an idea but as a person. [3]

> Blessed is the one who listens to *me*,
> watching daily at *my* gates,
> waiting beside *my* doors (Prov. 8:34).

Wisdom is likened to a person who loves us and whom we love. "I love those who love me," wisdom says (Prov. 8:17). Those "who hate me" injure themselves (Prov. 8:36; see also Prov. 8:20-21). To grow wiser in heart, we must pursue wisdom as we would a person, relationally and with love.

In this book, biblical sages invite us into this relationship of love. This isn't a book that merely gathers up ideas into abstraction so that we can reduce these ideas into leverageable bullet points that we can systematically manage for a more efficient, productive, and successful transaction with life.

In this book, we will follow the lead of the earliest Christians, and love Jesus as the true person of understanding. Jesus is the boy beneath the Wisemen-star who "increased in wisdom" (Luke 2:52). He intends to give all who follow him "a mouth and wisdom" (Luke 21:15). Jesus invites "all who would listen" to become his "disciple and enter his unique school of wisdom."[4] Jesus stands for all to hear and says of Himself, "Behold, something greater than Solomon is here" (Matt. 12:42). Jesus is not only "our wisdom" but "wisdom itself."[5]

Mark this down. Whenever we ask for wisdom, it's Jesus we ask for.

Consequently, when you finish this book, you'll have spent time with the person of Jesus, savoring His wisdom, relishing His love, and tasting the mouth-watering flavors of His life-changing graces.

The Posture of Wisdom
But to experience the person of Jesus as our wisdom, He'll want to teach us a listening posture.

> Blessed is *the one who listens* to me,
> *watching daily* at my gates,
> waiting beside my doors (Prov. 8:34).

Are you familiar with the game Connect Four? The game invites two players to be the first to align four colored checker pieces in a row. My five-year-old sees that he has two of his red pieces in a row and is about to place his third.

"Slow down," I say gently. "Step back. Take a longer look."

He sits back and furrows his little brows. He's focusing now.

"Oh!" he says, "I didn't see that."

He places his red piece to thwart my next move.

My three yellow pieces had shone brightly in front of him. But speedy looking rarely possesses the resources to grasp important patterns in plain sight.

Two days after playing Connect Four together, I was the student who needed to recover a posture more capable of seeing. Red raspberries and green grapes dotted my five-year-old's lunch plate.

Feeling hurried, I said, "Go ahead and eat buddy."

"I can't Daddy. I wuv the design."

"What design?" I asked. "You just need to go ahead and eat."

"But I can't Daddy. I wuv the design. See it. See it."

"We just need to get going, my man," I said.

He saddened. His eyes watered.

"*See* it Daddy! *See* it!"

I looked again at his plate. The red and green berries, with their differing bumpled and rounded shapes, had created a pleasing order and pattern of colors. Noah discerned a work of art on his lunch plate. It had his attention and gave him enjoyment. He wanted to linger over and enjoy his food before he ate it. My hurry to check off the task left me with no resources to notice or appreciate the pleasing array of colors and shapes Noah was relishing.

"He who has ears to hear, let him hear," Jesus says. He contrasts a kind of hearing that only reaches our ears, with a hearing that attends deeper with understanding. Paradoxically, we grow quieter, but our hearing amplifies, and our seeing grows more vivid.

If teachable to wisdom's posture, we'll begin to find it more possible to say as a poet did, "Now the ears of my ears are awake, now the eyes of my eyes are opened."[6]

The Pace of Wisdom

But we'll find this attentive posture of wisdom hard to practice unless we, by His grace, learn to trust wisdom's pace.

> Blessed is the one who listens to me,
> > watching daily at my gates,
> > *waiting* beside my doors (Prov. 8:34).

Unlike the mountain when skiing, the speed of wisdom is slow. "Waiting" is a patient thing.

You'll want to prepare yourself for the pace of this book. If reading this book hurries you into motion rather than slows you into meditation, your reading will work against the wisdom you seek.

Think of this book, then, not as a highway but as a country town road. A highway enables us to speed from one place to another. Its speed dissuades us from noticing the houses or tending to people or places we pass by. In contrast, a country town road slows one into noticing what's there.

By the end of this book, your inner life will find itself quieter. The inability of impatience to carry the wiser resources of God's grace will grow more visible to you. The treasures found by a patient way of handling time will be more valuable to you.

Wisdom is a Prayer

In this book, I want to help you grow wiser with life skills (part two). To do that, we'll first need to grow wiser with people, including ourselves (part one). But both endeavors will invite us to prayer.

Like the biblically wise before Him (Prov. 2:1-6) and His disciples after Him (James 1:5), Jesus teaches His students to bathe their pursuit of wisdom in prayer (Matt. 7:7-12).

Perhaps we want to grow wiser but haven't counted on our need to surrender to a person, a posture, a pace, *and prayer* to find it.

Take heart. Remember. Even though I tumbled on the mountain, a wise guide stayed with me. Moreover, a community of worried friends celebrated my return. Biblical wisdom, like proverbs, was given "as a manual to be worked through in a community of learners, with older, wiser mentors."[7] Biblical wisdom isn't sought as an isolated adventure out there on our own, but within a company of fellow wisdom seekers looking to Jesus, day by day.

Our next chapter awaits us now, providing access to your wisdom story and mine. But before we turn to receive the change that is about to begin within us, I've written what an earlier era of Christians called "a traveler's prayer." Pause here. Let's pray together.

Jesus, you are the wisdom of God.
The God whose wisdom I love.
I'm forsaken, foolish, a fraud.
Lest you guide me below and above.

Be mine in every thought, this day.
My words made wiser by yours.
Be mine in every step, I pray.
My heart, your wisdom secures. Amen.

Part One

Relationally Wiser with Jesus

1

Your Wisdom Story and Mine

*How old are we? As a culture, as individuals?
Not in years but wisdom.[8]*

As we take this first step into your wisdom story and mine, I feel like one sifting through a damp closet box, looking at three faded photos in my mind.

My first faded memory is Mom. She's twenty-one, crying on a bed. I'm an "out of wedlock," toddler standing off-balance in the hallway of an empty house of sorrows.

Two years later, maybe three, I remember smiling adults among candle flames and birthday balloons. They encouraged me to look to the light and wish for good.

These bed tears and birth songs occur next door to the church where my third earliest memory resides: a bush of wasps near the front door.

I want to help you grow "wise of heart" (Prov. 10:8; 16:21, 23); to experience healthier relationships, and make better decisions. I want to help you handle time in a more soul-satisfying way, and to invigorate your life purpose with an abiding sense of God's steadfast love.

But you should know at the outset, I've been naive and foolish, a latecomer to wiser things. I'm the diapered boy from the crying house. I'm the paper-hatted kid daring to make a wish and afraid I'll blow it. I'm the child who went to church and got stung.

I'm writing to you, not as one "looking at" my wisdom story as if standing distant and outside of it. But in the style of Ecclesiastes, Job or the wisdom Psalms, I'm sharing my wisdom story as one who "looks along" it from inside the experience, in the hope that in my story you'll discover a mirror of your own.[9] By "wisdom story," I refer to our experiences with wisdom or its absence throughout the scenes of our lives.

Wisdom at Home, in our Culture and at Church

Many fine folks grew up wonderfully as a child in wisdom's house (Luke 7:35). But wisdom wasn't part of my family's talk.

Sure. My Papaw might say, "Don't get too big for your britches." Or we'd sing of the three kings each Christmas and hang their pictures on the tree. But back they'd go into the basement box. Sage travelers were holiday ornaments, not mentors for living.

Similarly, wisdom didn't feature in the songs my generation listened to, the movies we watched, the classrooms we learned in, or the workrooms where we earned paychecks. Nothing within my heart considered this problematic. A children's story lamented the "old city of wisdom," in disrepair with "no one to set it right."[10] But like lint in my pocket, if wisdom traveled with me, I didn't know it.[11]

This wisdom deficit permeated church, too.

- Preachers were prophets, not sages.[12] We didn't ponder Jesus' description of his communicators as "prophets *and wise men* ..." (Matt. 23:34).[13] The idea that a preacher is a sage and the sermon a wisdom text never occurred to us.

- Theologically,[14] Jesus wonderfully fulfilled Old Testament voices like the prophet, priest, and king, but One Greater than Solomon (Matt. 12:42), the fulfillment of wisdom, and wisdom itself (1 Cor. 1:30; Col. 2:3) wasn't taught.[15]
- In our apologetics, we answered doubts like the problem of evil by debating Epicurus' syllogism, seemingly unaware that Jesus addressed this anguished question with a wisdom story. "Once upon a time, there was a farmer ..." (Matt. 13:24-30).[16]
- I tasted Jesus' "wisdom of the cross," knowing Him as the savior of my sins, Lord of my life, and friend for my loneliness. But less prominent was Jesus as creator, sustainer, and pre-eminent expert regarding every piece of reality, seen and unseen, anywhere, any time (Col. 1:15-17).

The Devastating Consequence

The result is that a whole batch of us grew up with no one saying:

> Get wisdom, nothing you desire can compare to her ...
> Get wisdom. Though it cost all you have ...
> (Prov. 3:13-18; 4:7; 16:16, NIV).

So, I was shocked the first time I read Augustine's Enchiridion, which said any Christian aspiring to faith, hope, and love must first become a wise person.[17] I was years into my life and ministry before it dawned upon me to cry out:

I AM A FOOL.

I lay on the floor, heaving beneath shelves of Jesus books, behind a desk on which an engraved ordination gift announced my job and name, "Pastor Zack."

But being Christian and spiritually gifted doesn't make one wise, and I hope you're beginning to see I'm not just talking about my wisdom story now, but yours.

If you've experienced a wisdom absence like mine, one consequence is that a whole cohort of Christians have been reading the Bible, creating art, working, making decisions, managing time, and responding to cultural questions, as a people severely undernourished by the Bible's Wisdom Literature (Job, Proverbs, Ecclesiastes, the Wisdom Psalms, and James[18]), and by the Bible *as* wisdom literature,[19] with little conscious awareness either way that Jesus is our wisdom.

What does it reveal about the conditions of our living rooms, workplaces, worship spaces, neighborhoods, and media platforms if most Christians today are engaging family, church, and culture out of a wisdom deficit?

A clue to the devastating importance of this question arises when we remember five core life environments and ask ourselves to what degree biblical wisdom saturates each one.

1. *Personal Life:* how we relate to our body and soul.

2. *Family/Friends Life:* including being parented, single, married, or parenting others, along with births, deaths, holidays, disagreements, and celebrations.

3. *Work Life:* how we relate to our aspirations, skills, education, role, colleagues, bosses, effort, rest, ambition, and money.

4. *Neighborhood Life*: how we relate to strangers, foreigners, other religions, national tragedies, cultural movements, philosophies, laws, hard questions and the physical environments of beauty and artistry in God's creation.

5. *Congregational life:* how we relate to worship, worship spaces, church people, church teachings, and church leaders.

Mark this down. Being wiser with Jesus in one area of life doesn't mean we're wise in every area of life. A skilled pastor can be simultaneously wise with the Bible (church life), naive with the opposite sex (personal/family/friendship life), foolish with fellow workers (work life), and tempted to scoff with other-than-Christian people (neighborhood life).

To help us grow wiser of heart, biblical sages ask their novices to cultivate greater attentiveness to the companions and houses featured within our lives. By tracing our companions and houses, the One Greater than Solomon can open our eyes to the wisdom story we've known and the wisdom repair God has for us.

Wisdom 101 is about to start. Let's take some notes together.

Discerning our Companions

First, every person encounters three kinds of people in life.

1. simple ones (naive)
2. scoffers
3. fools

> How long, *O simple ones*, will you love being *simple*?
> How long will *scoffers* delight in their *scoffing*
> and *fools* hate knowledge (Prov. 1:22)?

Our inability to discern these companions causes much of what hurts us (and most of the hurt we cause others). The wise teach students to recognize which kind of person is with them (and within them) and how wisdom responds accordingly.

In our next chapter, we'll begin exploring how Jesus relates to each of these differing companions. But for now, take note.

> Whoever walks with the wise becomes wise,
> but the companion of fools will *suffer harm* (Prov. 13:20).

Much of our suffering comes from living with a fool we deemed wise (or being the fool we thought wise). Our point? When Jesus describes one who is foolish (Luke 12:20), He isn't speaking in generalities or using off-hand slang, but describing a category of person, based on a set of ancient wisdom criteria.

Discerning our Houses

Next, the wise remind us that companions come from homes. When Jesus describes wise and foolish houses (Matt. 7:24-27), He continues this ancient wisdom metaphor for training students (Prov. 14:1; 24:3-4).[20] Houses, like all institutional cultures, reveal habits and ways of being.

Take a moment. Read and compare each verse on the left with the one on the right. No need to go too deep here, not yet. A glance will suffice.

Wisdom's House Culture	Folly's House Culture
Proverbs 9:1–6	Proverbs 9:13–18
[1] Wisdom has built her house; she has hewn her seven pillars.	[13] The woman Folly is loud; she is seductive and knows nothing.
[2] She has slaughtered her beasts; she has mixed her wine; she has also set her table.	[14] She sits at the door of her house; she takes a seat on the highest places of the town,
[3] She has sent out her young women to call from the highest places in the town,	[15] calling to those who pass by, who are going straight on their way,
[4] "Whoever is simple, let him turn in here!" To him who lacks sense she says,	[16] "Whoever is simple, let him turn in here!" And to him who lacks sense she says,
[5] "Come, eat of my bread and drink of the wine I have mixed.	[17] "Stolen water is sweet, and bread eaten in secret is pleasant."
[6] Leave your simple ways, and live, and walk in the way of insight."	[18] But he does not know that the dead are there, that her guests are in the depths of Sheol.

with fellow workers (work life), and tempted to scoff with other-than-Christian people (neighborhood life).

To help us grow wiser of heart, biblical sages ask their novices to cultivate greater attentiveness to the companions and houses featured within our lives. By tracing our companions and houses, the One Greater than Solomon can open our eyes to the wisdom story we've known and the wisdom repair God has for us.

Wisdom 101 is about to start. Let's take some notes together.

Discerning our Companions

First, every person encounters three kinds of people in life.

1. simple ones (naive)
2. scoffers
3. fools

> How long, *O simple ones*, will you love being *simple*?
> How long will *scoffers* delight in their *scoffing*
> and *fools* hate knowledge (Prov. 1:22)?

Our inability to discern these companions causes much of what hurts us (and most of the hurt we cause others). The wise teach students to recognize which kind of person is with them (and within them) and how wisdom responds accordingly.

In our next chapter, we'll begin exploring how Jesus relates to each of these differing companions. But for now, take note.

> Whoever walks with the wise becomes wise,
> but the companion of fools will *suffer harm* (Prov. 13:20).

Much of our suffering comes from living with a fool we deemed wise (or being the fool we thought wise). Our point? When Jesus describes one who is foolish (Luke 12:20), He isn't speaking in generalities or using off-hand slang, but describing a category of person, based on a set of ancient wisdom criteria.

Discerning our Houses

Next, the wise remind us that companions come from homes. When Jesus describes wise and foolish houses (Matt. 7:24-27), He continues this ancient wisdom metaphor for training students (Prov. 14:1; 24:3-4).[20] Houses, like all institutional cultures, reveal habits and ways of being.

Take a moment. Read and compare each verse on the left with the one on the right. No need to go too deep here, not yet. A glance will suffice.

Wisdom's House Culture	Folly's House Culture
Proverbs 9:1–6	Proverbs 9:13–18
[1] Wisdom has built her house; she has hewn her seven pillars.	[13] The woman Folly is loud; she is seductive and knows nothing.
[2] She has slaughtered her beasts; she has mixed her wine; she has also set her table.	[14] She sits at the door of her house; she takes a seat on the highest places of the town,
[3] She has sent out her young women to call from the highest places in the town,	[15] calling to those who pass by, who are going straight on their way,
[4] "Whoever is simple, let him turn in here!" To him who lacks sense she says,	[16] "Whoever is simple, let him turn in here!" And to him who lacks sense she says,
[5] "Come, eat of my bread and drink of the wine I have mixed.	[17] "Stolen water is sweet, and bread eaten in secret is pleasant."
[6] Leave your simple ways, and live, and walk in the way of insight."	[18] But he does not know that the dead are there, that her guests are in the depths of Sheol.

The Cultures of Our Houses

Compare the two houses.

First, both houses preach the same message.

> Whoever is simple, let him turn in here! To him who lacks sense she says ... (vv. 4, 16).

But how can we discern wisdom from folly if both preach the same message and promise the same benefits?

"I'm glad you've asked," a sage teacher says. "You cannot tell by the messages and promises themselves. Just as in life, you must learn to pay closer attention to the subtle habits each house prizes and cultivates—the walk they offer within their talk."

For example, folly's house prizes self-preferencing talk (loud)[21] and tantalizing quick-fix experiences (seduction).[22] Though arrogantly ignorant of what it boasts (knows nothing), it possesses little curiosity or energy to learn otherwise (she sits) (vv. 13-14).

But while folly sits and jabbers about itself, wisdom quietly works, building and maintaining her house, tending animals, cooking food, mixing wine, and setting a table for guests.

Folly's House-Culture	Wisdom's House-Culture
Boastful	*Humble*
Immediate gratification	*Patient*
Hot air knowledge	*Seasoned knowledge*
Sits and steals	*Faithfully works*

Moreover, notice that folly lives a second-hand life. She possesses no first-hand quiet or faithful work of her own. Sweetness is something plagiarized, pulled into orbit to circle her (v. 17).

In contrast, the phrase "she has" repeats five times and reveals wisdom's abundance (vv. 1-3). Wisdom can say, "Come eat of *my* bread, the wine *I have* mixed" (v. 5).

Moreover, while folly positions her house to be seen by others (v. 14), wisdom's house remains contentedly out of sight. The wise easily find Lady Wisdom's address, but the unwise wouldn't imagine something so prized found in so humble a place. Because of this, fools search for wisdom in vain unless they have a change of heart (Prov. 14:6).

What's more, wisdom sends her apprentices to speak while she remains home to prepare (v. 3). Wisdom shares her life with others. She empowers them with dignity, trust, and a role to play.

In contrast, folly works alone, meets you outside the door, offers no table (v. 14) and hides what's inside her house. She gathers guests, but "they do not know the dead are there" (v. 18). How did they not know except that there was much in the house the foolish host keeps hidden?

The result? Words like "way," "live," and "walk" describe wisdom's house culture, whereas folly's house is built on nothing but talk (v. 6).

The Cultures of Our Leadership and Parenting

Consider a leader or parent trained by folly's house.

> They become a self-orbiting, quick-fix talker, thirsty for immediate experiences. They're often busy borrowing and leveraging the thoughts and works of others to prop up their own importance. They prize being first and known while rarely trusting or empowering others, unless those others loyally orbit around them. They talk much but have no soul-quiet of their own to offer. They offer only what is stolen or borrowed from others. Foolish ones are fully committed to preserving their own centrality and content with keeping

relationships in the dark while smiling and gathering a crowd at the front door. They place themselves where everyone can see them.

Now, imagine someone trained in wisdom's house.

A quiet worker, patient, knowledgeable, and skilled, who serves the community by persistently creating a hospitable welcome for grace-needy neighbors. They are less wise than they want to be but enjoy and cultivate sturdy and lasting delights, with hard-fought-for humility. They invite others by listening, mentoring, empowering, and entrusting those who will outshine them. They are content to embody artistry, architecture, and hospitable expertise for its own God-given joys. They are happy to live in an ordinary and overlooked part of town.

Finally, notice the difference between the intended audience of both houses.

For Lady Wisdom those *without* wisdom and insight lack sense (v. 6).

For Lady Folly, those *with* wisdom and insight lack sense. She targets those trying to go "straight on their way" (v. 15). Folly believes God's wisdom needs a fool's guidance.

Clarifying Our Definition of Wisdom

At this point, we pause. We're noticing that biblical sages teach wisdom by inviting our closer attentiveness to the ways of people and places.

Their focus surprised me at first. I knew that "the fear of the Lord" is where wisdom begins (Prov. 1:7; 9:10-12). Wisdom is something akin to what novelist Walker Percy called, "the search."[23] A worldview we use to frame the world. A meaningful story we tell by which to make sense of things.

I also began to have an inkling of wisdom as a Mystery skill; what filmmaker Taika Waititi called, "the knack."[24] The skill set capable of puzzling together knowns to successfully navigate unknowns (Eccles. 8:5-6).

But I was nearly a half-century old before learning that wisdom is also a love, kin to what John Donne called "the captiv'd heart."[25]

Jesus is the truth (our worldview).

Jesus is the way (the skilled one we follow).

But Jesus is also the life (John 14:6). He animates, drives, and satisfies us.

To keep us from merely describing wise people as those who fear the Lord and who know how to avoid the wrong houses and companions, biblical sages confront our inner lives.

For them, wisdom is a love. We locate the wise, not merely by recognizing those who say accurate sentences doctrinally (as important as true sentences are), or have a biblical skill set (as thankful as we are for that), but by noticing what one loves, as they relate to people, to themselves, to the world, and to God.

Introducing our Loves

Look again at the wisdom text, which introduced us to life's companions.

> How long, O simple ones, will you *love* being simple?
> How long will scoffers *delight* in their scoffing
> and fools *hate* knowledge (Prov. 1:22)?

Notice.

A naive heart *loves* naivete.

A scoffer *delights* in scoffing.

A fool *hates* wise knowledge.

Imagine a work team spiraling six months after a new hire. The new worker aligns with the company's worldview (the search) and is skilled prudently (the knack). But his arrival has created unnecessary conflict and pain. Why? He finds folly enthralling (captiv'd heart).

> Trusting a fool to convey a message
> is like cutting off one's feet or drinking poison ...
> An employer who hires a fool or a bystander
> is like an archer who shoots at random (Prov. 26:6, 10 NLT).

The worker in his proverb is vision-aligned and skilled. Why then is there a problem? The worker loves folly. He delights in quick-fix talk, boasts about what he doesn't know, reacts without listening. People get hurt for no rational reason (like an archer who shoots at random) and company vision derails (like cutting off one's feet).

What if Sages Aren't Our Kind of People?

When pondering the companions, houses, and loves of my life, I've had to admit a disorienting realization. Sages haven't been my kind of people.

- A biblical sage finds it no waste of time to orient her gaze toward a star; to stare hours at ants or a field, a lily, or a bird, as if created things can teach us God-given truths (Prov. 6:6, 24:30-32; Matt. 6:26).

- A biblical sage believes that God prizes truth and equity and that falsehood, injustice, and evil exist.

- A biblical sage will quote what is true and good, regardless of who said it. They'll light up the dark with their candle even if a fool provides the match.[26]

- A biblical sage often speaks with first-hand experience, from inside the way things are. They say things like: "Come let us get drunk with love," or "I hated life." They talk about pain like those who howl and vomit. They talk about beauty as those ravaged by pleasure or who wish they could be (Eccles. 2:17-18; Song 5:1).

- Not all loves are wise. A person can believe rightly and act skillfully, while naive at home, foolish with workers, and a scoffer in the neighborhood.

One Greater than Solomon Has Come

After taking these notes and walking outside after our first wisdom class together, we might feel humbled, even disheartened. "I will never find wisdom. I'm a failure at everything."[27]

But grace reminds us of two hopes.

Hope number one is that wisdom's table is set for the wisdom-failed.

> Whoever is simple, let him turn in here!" To him who lacks sense she says,
> Come, eat of my bread ... (Prov. 9:4-5).

What the old sages foreshadowed, Jesus fulfills.

> Come to me, all who labor and are heavy laden and I will give you rest (Matt. 11:28).
>
> I am the bread of life (John 6:35).

Hope number two is that while harm comes to us relationally (a companion of fools suffers harm) so does healing (walk with the wise and become wise).

In eighth grade football, coach J called time out.

"What's the play, Eswine?"

I called a play featuring David's skills. We won the championship.

The next school day, Coach M, the basketball coach, sought me out.

"I heard Coach J left the game in your hands."

"Yes, sir," I answered.

"What a dumb ass!" he said. "I'd never do that. You don't have what it takes to lead, son. Don't you forget it."

Perhaps this coach delighted like a scoffer to knife-rip a kid's blue-ribbon moments. Maybe he loved folly's growl when training young men. Perhaps he disliked the football coach and misplaced his anger from a crushed spirit. Or maybe he later regretted it but didn't know how to ask a fourteen-year-old's forgiveness in the hallways of our Christian school.

What I do know now is that his problem wasn't worldview (*Christian* coach) or skill set (*winning* coach), but heart-loves and their relational outworking. Accumulate enough moments like these and you begin to curl up and quit or cry out and rage at the world.

But wisdom repair often arrives in what looks on the surface like similar packages but, beneath, the wrappings are nothing alike.

Decades later, I'd just finished lunch with Professor J in a Christian graduate school.

"Shall I take our plates to your secretary?" I asked.

"Zack," he said kindly, "my secretary is not our maid. We mustn't treat her as such. We can take our own dishes to the sink and wash them ourselves."[28]

We washed our dishes together and met the day with laughter.

My point?

Early on, one man saw good and tore me down.

Later on, another man saw fault but helped me up.

Somehow, within scenes like these from the dark script of my foolish, broken-apart life, One Greater than Solomon was walking with me. "Let there be light," he said. And by the cruciform grace, there was.

Wherever you are and whatever you've been through, the porch lamp of wisdom's house hasn't dimmed. It still glows for you. I smell fresh baked bread warming. I hear belly-laugh rest, an invitation to wiser tears and kinder loves. I'm heading there now and I'm asking you to come with me.

2

When We're Naive

"We worship the happy face."[29]

Perhaps you've heard the tale of Snow White. She bites an apple offered by an old hag, not knowing it was poisoned.

In older versions, the poisoned apple marks her third temptation.

First, the hag strangles Snow with lace.

Second, the witch hexes Snow with a comb.

Both times, Snow's friends rescue her from death.

Now, we arrive at the third knock on the door and the apple shining tastily before us.

> "I cannot let anyone in," Snow says, "they've forbidden me!"
> (Notice, that instead of seeing it wise to boundary this witch, Snow blames her friends).
>
> "Are you afraid of poison?" asks the old woman.

Any of us who witnessed the lace and the comb cry out, YES! WE ARE AFRAID OF POISON!

But not Snow. She finds a smiling evil more reliable than the hard data of past experience and the good counsel of concerned friends.

> "Look," the sorceress says, "I'll cut the apple in two. You eat the red side, and I'll eat the white."

By now, we're yelling, RUN GIRL! RUN FOR YOUR LIFE! But Snow doesn't run. We all know what happens next.[30]

Why Naive Hearts Look Wise for a While
"Naive," as used in the Proverbs, means "open."[31] Inviting a naive heart to begin a romantic relationship or small group couldn't be better.

> Do you want Chinese food or pizza tonight?
>
> "Whatever!" says naivete. "It's all good."
>
> "Do you mind if we believe this or that, act this way and not that way?"
>
> "Whatever!" says naivete. "I'm open!"

Openness is wise (James 3:17). Naive hearts resemble the wise who dance, believe, embrace (Eccles. 3:1-8), and laugh (Prov. 17:22). As we'll discover, if you've been face-slapped by the strobe-light emotions of a fool or wonder-robbed by the cynical meanness of a scoffer, you'll be glad for the soothing rest naive company provides.

The problem with naivete isn't its openness, but its unwillingness to close the door, even when evil wants in.

> The simple believes everything,
> but the prudent gives thought to his steps (Prov. 14:15).

The Anatomy of a Naive Heart

A naive heart resists closing unwise doors because it values three unwise ways of relating (Rom. 16:18).

- *Smooth Words*: No climbing-hill-speech to fatigue the breath, or sore the muscles.
- *Flattery*: Honey-tongued with flies in the heart.
- *Shiny experiences that deceive*: Sugary lies.

These relational preferences enable naive hearts to say:

1. *We're all good.* Shiny syllables keep things easy, romantic, answered.

2. *I feel good.* Sweet talk enamors us.

3. *Why talk about it?* It will ruin the vibe.

If naivete were a fly, it would resist expressing its dislike of the spider's silky prison. Speaking this way would feel mean. Identifying one idea or person as truer or safer than another feels unloving, narrow, confining, and mood-killing. We wouldn't want the spider to think us close-minded.

> The prudent sees danger and hides himself,
> but the simple go on and suffer for it (Prov. 22:3; 27:12).

Jesus addresses this naive unwillingness to believe that hard things don't apply to them.

An architect envisions beauty in a once-barren place. A king envisions victory though outmatched. Both avoid what Jesus calls "counting the cost" (Luke 14:28-32). The architect leaves a building half-finished. The king loses a fight only wisdom could win.

What does Jesus see in a naive life that causes him to diagnose "cost counting" as the problem?

Naive hearts trust quick fixes.
"Whoever sings songs to a heavy heart is like one who takes off a garment on a cold day, and like vinegar on soda" (Prov. 25:20).

"Are you cold? Surely, it's not as bad as you make it. Here, let me take your coat from you and you'll see."

To a naive mind, annoyances, pain, illness, trauma, or sins, should be easily overcome. Clueless to the pain our pleasantness causes, we not-so-helpfully say, "Let me add this vinegar to your soda. That's better now, isn't it?"

If you're a leader, naive critics won't ask, "What is the wise thing to do?" They'll ask, "What's the fastest way to make us feel good again and why aren't you doing that?"

A naive parent, sibling, or friend, will respond to your admission of fear, sorrow, or anxiety, not with empathy, but by curtly skipping over your discomfort and telling you why things are fine, like a pastor who quotes Bible verses with the smiling anticipation that "all is well now, isn't it?"

Naive hearts relish an immediate thrill.
"Whoever goes about slandering reveals secrets; therefore do not associate with a simple babbler" (Prov. 20:19). We'll tell a story that isn't ours, because it feels good and puts us center stage for the moment. To count the cost of such gossip would require us to forego the thrill of the spotlight and the inside scoop.

The immediate thrill renders a deeper look uninteresting to us, like two friends watching a food show. The wiser friend, says, "I wonder what they do with the extra food?"

"Shhh!" says the naive friend. "Just enjoy the show."

"I am," says the wiser friend. "I love the skill of these chefs. I'm just saying, what's it like for a person who experiences food scarcity to watch food used as entertainment?"

"Enough," says the naive friend, clicking off the television. "Let's get something to eat."

Naive hearts only learn the hard way.
Unless a scoffer is punished, the naive won't learn (Prov. 19:25). Because we've busied ourselves taking your coats and spoiling your sodas with happy songs, smiling Scriptures, and inspirational gifts, we're shocked if you suggest that our "help" makes things harder. We don't believe you. We know our happy tune is right. Snow opened the door three times and so will we. Like two young lovers putting a smile on anything cautionary in their relationship. It will take a hard consequence before we grow more honest and learn. Until then, we don't tend the weeds in the flowerbed and are surprised when the flowers wilt or die.

A naive heart rarely apologizes.
Not learning, we believe legitimate guilt doesn't fit with how open, nice, and helpful we are. If we do apologize, we use "sorry" to hurry us back to the good vibe. Our "sorry" carries a tone of hurried impatience rather than the regretful sadness of slowing down to humble ourselves for a wrong done to those we love.

* * *

A quick-fix, immediate-gratification, slow-to-learn, slow-to-apologize person could use wisdom's ability to feel negative costs and learn from them. A naive heart would create less unnecessary pain for itself and for others.

Consider a naive man leaves his wife and kids because "God wants him to be happy." That means his wife and kids must interpret God as inflicting them with the debilitating anxiety of abandonment that will off balance them the rest of their lives, in the name of keeping the man happy.

If the woman and children had the same privilege as the man—to have what most makes them happy—they'd want their family back. But this double standard wouldn't occur to a naive heart. It doesn't see itself bound by the same rules it requires of others.

His wife and kids cling to one another in ruins on the porch. He gets into his car and cheerfully says, "Don't worry. We'll still be friends. Who knows? Maybe we'll get back together someday?"

Mark this down. Wiser hearts weep with those who weep. But our naive hearts try to cheer up, quick-fix, or rejoice with those who weep. For all its mirth, a naive heart robs us of our tears.

A Case Study in Naive Relating

Elkanah loved his wife, Hannah. Hannah is womb-barren—experiencing the shattered dream of motherhood. A rival woman repeatedly re-tears the scabs of Hannah's wounds. Hannah has "church hurt," slandered by foolish clergy. The dam breaks. Tears of sorrow flood her life.

Elkanah responds.

> Hannah, why do you weep? And why do you not eat? And why is your heart sad? Am I not more to you than ten sons (1 Sam. 1:7-8)?

Notice Elkanah's response.

Elkanah responds in a self-referential way, ... re-orbitting Hannah's sorrows around himself. Rather than stepping into her shoes, he wears his and wonders why she won't smile and dance. He offers a smiling remedy (his romantic love) that has nothing to do with the cause of her tears (barren, abused, slandered).

But Elkanah also responds by reducing Hannah's sorrows. He assumes that a happiness in one area of Hannah's life (romantic love with him) should minimize the sorrows in others (her other relational pains, her shattered dream of a child, her experience with church hurt). Elkanah naively underestimates the nuance of sorrow and joy, existing simultaneously, within the same person.

Moreover, Elkanah remains clueless to his own painful contribution. After all, Hannah's cruel provocateur is Elkanah's other wife. He could enter that pain to advocate for Hannah, but he either doesn't see it or avoids it, viewing himself as more innocent, nice, and bright than is warranted.

Consequently, when Hannah weeps she weeps alone. She must bear with Elkanah's painful implication that her sorrows minimize him and his love. She must comfort Elkanah, to prove her love for him as if he is the pained one. The result of Elkanah's "help" only furthers Hannah's plight.

My point?

Naive hearts steal our tears and then tell us to cheer up.

Or they steal our tears and then tear up.

Either way, when a naive heart hurts us, it cluelessly wonders why we're hurt.

The naive heart forgets that those who make light of hardships create them.

It remains true that naive hearts delight us in the beginning. New beginnings are their strength.

"Would you like Chinese food or pizza tonight?"

"Whatever," they say. "It's all good."

But six months or six years into this, the pain seeps in.

"I just want to know your opinion," we say. "It's only dinner."

"Come on," says naivete. "Let's watch that show you like. That'll be nice, right?"

"No. Please. I'm feeling hurt. Why is this so hard? I feel like I'm the one always having to make this decision." Or "Your voice matters as a teammate. I want to know your mind."

At this, naive smiles and jokes or bursts into a punishing or pouting silent treatment. Or maybe it floods the floor with childish tears and demands that you comfort it.

Either way, without wisdom, blame suddenly shifts to you. You gently asked a naive heart for a wisdom step, and to your surprise, a wisdom step is the one thing in life the naive are not open to (Prov. 1:32). They have no imagination yet for how God might weep with them within the unanswered negativities of a day.

As we'll see in chapter five, sometimes what presents itself as naivete arises from a wound after having been sinned against.

But whether naive or wounded, we get to discover with Hannah, that unlike the women, men, and clergy in her life, God saw her, heard her, and entered her sorrows.

One Greater than Solomon Has Come

But if our hearts love naivete, what hope do we have?

To answer this life-changing question, we look to Jesus, the person of understanding.

By a well, Jesus invited a naive heart to follow Him. His way with this woman reveals His healing path of discipleship for naive hearts. If we pay attention, He'll show us how we can more wisely relate to naive hearts (and how He intends to reach us in our own naivete).

To begin, *Jesus invites a naive heart into human vulnerability (John 4:7).* He is tired, thirsty, and not hiding His human limits, but asking if she might help Him. Naive openness dislikes feeling limited, messy or needy. But to reach you, Jesus invites you into what is limited, vulnerable, and human.

Jesus invites a naive heart into cultural sorrows (John 4:9). He is Jewish, a man. She's a Samaritan, a woman. As we'll see in our next chapter, a foolish heart would convert a landmine conversation like this into attack. Fools aren't open to conversation amid ethnic, political, and theological differences. Only an impartial soul can do this (James 3:17). This woman proves the genuineness of her openness by following Jesus into this volatile cultural terrain. To reach your naive heart, Jesus will enter the uncomfortable tensions within your life and generation.

Then, *Jesus invites a naive heart with wonder (John 4:10-15).* There amid fatigue, thirst, human limits, cultural and ethnic sorrows, Jesus says, "I know of a water that lives."

A foolish or scoffing heart would immediately dismiss this appeal to wonder; finding it childish and unfit for the real world, too trite for real theology.

But wisdom, though it sheds naive openness, never lets go of childlike wonder (Mark 10:15).

> There is much evil in the world, yet everything is not evil. The setting sun, the wings of a butterfly and the song of the wind—these are good and the heart knows it.[32]

Can you believe enchantment exists, something fantastic, a realm unseen and alongside this physical world, so near we can almost touch it? The woman can. "Tell me," she says, "where is this breathing water? I'd be glad for a taste of it."

Now, *Jesus invites a naive heart to admit personal sorrows (John 4:16),* which puts naivete at a crossroads. If you want to know what a naive heart will need to grow wiser with Jesus, slow down now. Pay attention here.

"Go call your husband," Jesus says. The woman responds with naive skill: "I have no husband." She tells a truth that lies. She surface-talks to keep the mood light and avoids the deep wreckage beneath. She tries maneuvering Jesus toward the same.

But Jesus is not naive. He is unlike anyone she's ever met. Wisdom knows how to wade into the bog waters of our pains, and weep with us.

> You are right in saying, 'I have no husband'; for you have had five husbands, and the one you now have is not your husband. What you have said is true (John 4:17-18).

Most naive hearts end the conversation here. Jesus holds up a mirror of hard, sorrowing things that darken the mood, kill the vibe, and require her to begin counting the cost of her life.

If Jesus asks you to see what brings the vibe down and makes the mood heavy in your life, can you trust Him? She risks it.

"I perceive that you are a prophet," she says. Perhaps more than a prophet, the promised one of old.

Grace upon grace. She doesn't close the door. At her willingness to reframe their conversation and place it into God's explicit presence, *Jesus invites the naive heart to Himself.*

"I am He."

Another crossroads.

Jesus is not *a* truth, but *the* truth. Not *a* savior, but *the* Savior. She must interpret everything personal and anything cultural whether Jewish, Samaritan or Gentile, in Jesus' light and named as Jesus would name it. Jesus exposes all other rival loves as forgeries by comparison, and she must confess this and close the door to them.

Naive hearts who make it this far with Jesus often go no further. When Jesus says He's *the* Messiah, rather than one among many, it feels mean, narrow, bigoted, and unkind.

But the woman at the well discovers the opposite. She demonstrates the power of a naive heart when it begins to trust that Jesus is *the* truth, *the* way, *the* life. Her openness, now transformed by wiser love, frees her to do what most never will. Tell anyone anywhere about Jesus.

Hope for the Naive Heart
Is there hope for a naive heart? Yes!

> The LORD preserves the simple;
> when I was brought low, he saved me (Ps. 116:6).

But hope for the naive comes by being led to the place we've resisted going. The "brought low," place with the Lord.

Our naivete can't imagine Jesus in the "brought low" places. We picture Jesus as naive like us—committed to unlimited good moods and using all His power to minimize negative feelings or costly circumstances. Jesus, as we imagine Him, resists anything that would bring down the vibe, limit our options, or require us to face hardship for the good of another.

So, our naive hearts quote "take heart; Jesus has overcome the world!" but forget how Jesus began the sentence. "In the world, you will have tribulation" (John 16:33).

Naive hearts need to learn how to cry about crying things.

- Jesus cried for His friends when one of them died. A naive heart imagines saying to Jesus, "No need to cry; it'll be fine." But the one who'll make it fine is the One Greater than Solomon. He weeps His own tears. He joins the tears of others. His tears reveal His love (John 11:35), as ours do. Love entering the "brought low" places is what the wise seek.

- Jesus cried for His enemies when the city, the people, and the generation in which He lived, rejected Him (Luke 19:41).

- Jesus cried when counting the cost of His Father's good purpose for His life (Heb. 5:7).

Jesus' enemies, friends, and heavenly Father saw Jesus' tears and heard Him cry.

Our naive heart pictures Jesus as a jolly man of whimsy, unaware that, though full of joy (John 15:11; 17:13, 24-26), Jesus is, like any wise person, "a man of sorrows and acquainted with grief" (Isa. 53:3).

The earliest Christians found comfort here. Jesus was tempted, broken, and hurt in every way that we are. He went to the "brought low" places without sinning, so that we who must go there too have an advocate of mercy, who knows first-hand how to help in our times of need (Heb. 2:14-18; 4:15-16).

Tasting this advocacy in the brought low places, the earliest Christians began to speak of God as their comforter, "who comforts us in all our affliction." Wisdom gives us the capacity "to comfort those in any affliction, with the comfort" God has given us (2 Cor. 1:3-4).

The true wisdom deficit of naivete surfaces here. Though open and able to laugh and wonder, a naive heart has neither the relational resources to enter the real sorrows of life nor the non-trite comforts of God to offer those crushed by tearful places. A naive heart wouldn't know what to do with days of silence and torn clothes in Job's presence. It struggles to imagine the cross of Jesus as God's wisdom way—sacrifice, suffering, entering the "brought low" places of sin and being sinned against.

But Jesus, the man of sorrows, enters life's mourning places. Out of love, He feistily declares "Blessed" to those He finds there (Matt. 5:4).

Christ the Prudent

So, if our hearts are naive, the discipleship Jesus invites us to will include our need to count the cost and learn the wisdom of prudence.

> O simple ones, learn prudence (Prov. 8:5)!

Prudence reflects that aspect of God's character by which He enters the uncomfortable discernment of persons, work, words, and emotions (Prov. 10:5, 19; 12:16, 23; 14:8). We grow astute to discern which doors to close and which to keep unblocked. Wisdom calls for "a discernment of cries," prudent to distinguish cries of amazement and gratitude from cries of boredom or misuse.[33]

There's a reason "the simple inherit folly" (Prov. 14:18). The witch, like all scoffers and fools, depends upon Snow's naivete. For all its openness, naivete allows folly to mentor it and becomes its benefactor. Naivete never stands in folly's way.

No wonder the cross of Jesus becomes dear to once naive hearts.

There, Jesus died to free us from our self-referential, reductionistic, blindspot-blind, quick-fixes. He un-enslaved us from our lament-skipping, gullible protectiveness of folly that has so damaged us and those we love.

But the grace. The grace! Wisdom has built her house for simpletons like us. She set her table, sent out her invitations, and urges all who are naive to come enjoy her hospitality, to learn her ways.

> Whoever is simple, let him turn in here!
> ... Come, eat of my bread
> and drink of the wine I have mixed.
> Leave your simple ways, and live,
> and walk in the way of insight (Prov. 9:4-6).

And what is this way of insight we learn to walk but knowledge of the Holy One (Prov. 9:10).

And how is this knowledge gained?

"Follow me," Jesus says.

For all the times you've skipped over lament and tried to rejoice with those who weep.

For all the times you've denied prudence, opened harm's door, suffered unnecessary harm and caused it.

For all the times you've avoided genuine apology and required others to comfort you for the hurt you've created.

For all the times you've resisted cost-counting and left a hard good undone.

"I forgive you," says the One Greater than Solomon.

Now come to me.

Apprentice with me for I am prudence.

Learn from me. I am the wisdom of weeping.

3

When We're Foolish

What kind of mind is odder than his who mists a mirror and then complains that it's not clear.[34]

A child fails at climbing up a couch and cries.
"Stop your crying," Dad says, striding forcefully toward the child.
"I think I'd cry too."
The dad stops mid-stride.
"What?"
"The boy's legs are little. The couch is big," I say.
The man stares at me.
"When I try hard but fail," I say, "I feel frustrated too, even angry. Sometimes I cry."
"Go on," the man says.
"Defiance is real. But what if *this* isn't *that*?"
The man pauses. "You mean, he's frustrated?"
"Tenacious too. Look how many times he's tried and failed since we sat down."
The man's face relaxes. He lifts the child into a crawl over the couch ledge. The child smiles through his tears and the man sits down bewildered.

"What just happened?" he says.

"We just reminded ourselves that children feel angry, sad, frightened, and frustrated just like we all do, and often for good reasons. Frustration at a failed effort is not defiance of a parent."

***

Parents aren't the only ones capable of misinterpreting a negative emotion. In our last chapter, we noted Elkanah's naive response to Hannah. But when Eli the clergyman saw Hannah's tears, he responded to her with the characteristics of a foolish heart. He asked his congregant no questions and relied solely on his own reactive mind. Instead of weeping with Hannah, Eli wrongly rebuked her (1 Sam. 1:12-14).

Leaders can misinterpret people too. King Rehoboam's followers needed rest. They asked the new king for it and pledged their earnest work afterward.

Wise counselors said something like:

Humble yourself
Listen to understand
Respond kindly
Enact a patient plan
Trust will deepen, the kingdom will flourish
You'll delight in your people
They'll bless you.

But Rehoboam's younger counselors reacted negatively to this wise counsel. Rehoboam must show them who's boss, deny their request, and let them know they don't yet know what it's like to work, but he will make sure they learn.

Folly forgets that a request for a break needn't derive from foul motives. Human beings have limits. They make honest mistakes. We get frustrated by frustrating things, are saddened by sad things, worn out by wearying things, and all this with no intention to attack, mislead, or harm.

Rehoboam listens to the foolish advice of his younger advisors. An attentive pace of rest and work toward a long-term vision seemed weak and disrespectful to them.

Wisdom says. "If you've been foolish, exalting yourself ... put your hand on your mouth." For just as "pressing the nose produces blood ... pressing anger produces strife" (Prov. 30:32-33).

Rehoboam refused to cover folly's mouth. He bloodied the nose and lost half his kingdom (1 Kings 12).

Anatomy of a Foolish Heart

If naivete robs our tears, folly unnecessarily multiplies them.

If naivete avoids conflict, folly doesn't know what to do without it. Anger lodges within its heart (Eccles. 7:9; Prov. 18:6 19:12, 20:2), making it lion-like, easily provoked into baring teeth and growling.

"I've got an idea!" we say.
"Grrrr," says folly.

"I feel hurt."
Grrrr.

"I disagree."
Grrrr.

"Happy Birthday!"
Grrrr.

Why does folly misinterpret others and increase unnecessary pain?

1. Folly is neither curious nor teachable with your opinions.

A fool takes no pleasure in understanding, but only in expressing his opinion (Prov. 18:2; 12:15; 15:5, 14).

Folly's questions are masks worn by instructions and declarations.

A father begins narrating a story about his adult daughter. Four minutes in, you realize he, not his daughter, is the hero of this story. Fourteen minutes later, he adds a moral, advising you that his way is better than what most tell you these days.

For eighteen minutes now, you've been corralling a squirmy toddler on the verge of a meltdown for want of a nap. The eighteen minutes began because you said "hello" and mentioned your toddler daughter's fatigue while walking out the church door.

"I remember once, how my daughter needed a job," he began in response.

Our fool-hearted loved ones find no happiness in understanding us. They instruct when not asked. Moralize when hearing our experience. Curiosity to see what we see eludes them.

2. Folly reacts with disproportionate negative emotions.

> A fool gives full vent to his spirit, but a wise man quietly holds it back (Prov. 29:11).
>
> The vexation of a fool is known at once, but the prudent ignores an insult (Prov. 12:16; 14:17).

Set the table with the wrong forks, accidentally spill milk, or suggest a different opinion, and each receives "full vent." Conversations and emails require full rebuttal, word for word, line by line. No insults, perceived or real, are overlooked. Equal treatment for every perceived slight constantly makes ordinary easiness heavier than necessary (Prov. 27:3).

3. Folly doesn't apologize.

> Doing wrong is like a joke to a fool (Prov. 10:23).

Fools mock at the guilt offering (Prov. 14:9).

A fool's apology?
"I'm sorry *that you* misunderstood what I'm saying."
"I'm sorry *that you* think I was defensive."
"I'm sorry *that you* can't express yourself better."
Wisdom captures this unwillingness to admit fault with a courtroom example.

> A rebuke goes deeper into a man of understanding than a hundred blows into a fool (Prov. 17:10).

Count slowly to ten out loud or beneath your breath if you can.

1 confrontation of his wrongdoing
2 confrontations of his wrongdoing
3
4
5
6
7
8
9
10

Ninety more disciplinary confrontations and neither the fool's own pain, nor the pain he causes others softens his heart. Though vigilant with the slights of others, folly is complacent regarding its own folly (Prov. 1:32), untroubled by it, content to defend it (Prov. 26:11).

4. The result? Honest conversation about humbling or disagreeable things is nearly impossible.

> If a wise man has an argument with a fool, the fool only rages and laughs, and there is no quiet (Prov. 29:9).

Folly tries whichever emotional strategy will work to dislodge the wisdom you offer. It will joke with you, but quickly mood-swing growl, if you don't go along.

Folly demands the last word until it wins (Prov. 10:8, 10, 14; 18:6-7; 20:3). Given the choice to pursue a wiser relationship with you, folly shockingly prefers a strained relationship or none at all, while blaming you for it.

No wonder those who endure a Bible-quoting fool gradually grow cynical.

> Like a lame man's legs, which hang useless, is a proverb in the mouths of fools ...
> Like a thorn that goes up into the hand of a drunkard is a proverb in the mouth of fools (Prov. 26:7, 9).

Just as a thorn isn't felt and causes no response from a drunkard's hand, so truth on the lips of a fool makes no felt difference in the fool's life.[35] Folly quotes biblical truth but has no taste for biblical wisdom (Prov. 15:21; 21:20), preferring to adjust "the truth so he does not have to adjust to it."[36] Folly is wise in its own eyes (Prov. 12:15).

Naivete: rejoices with those who weep, can be jealous of those who rejoice.

Folly: instructs, corrects, admonishes those who weep, and rejoices only if those rejoicing agree with or preference it.

Jesus' Parables for the Foolish Heart

Consider ten bridesmaids, half of them wise, the others foolish (Matt. 25:1-13).[37] In Jesus' story, each bridesmaid is asked to bring a lamp and oil to light it, an understood custom at the time. Five of the maids brought lamps but no oil to light them. They demanded the bridal party remedy this situation for them and grew offended when "no" was the answer. This was not a case of forgetfulness but willfulness. These maids felt they weren't like the others and that customary expectations didn't apply to them.

- *When a foolish heart experiences self-inflicted hurts, it (a) blames others, (b) instructs them, (c) and demands their accommodation* (vv. 8-9).

- *If a foolish heart finally follows wisdom's counsel, stark consequences remain (v. 10).*

- *Fools instruct God, demanding that God act foolishly on their behalf* (vv. 11-12; Prov. 19:3).

In sum, folly creates a conflict where there isn't one. It makes what is asked of everyone (oil for a lamp) a personal offense.

For example, foolish in-laws treat the newly married couple as unloving and disloyal. They don't recognize that every newly married couple, not just *their* kids, and every parent, not just *them*, must learn to let go of and alter holiday traditions.

Or consider a mom, jealous of the woman who "took her boy." She relationally pursues her son without her daughter-in-law. For years the son goes along, excusing the pain his wife endures. Now with grown children of his own, the husband finally says "enough" and asks a sensible thing; that Mom and Dad extend dignity and inclusion to his wife.

His parents treat his sensible request with outrage, hurt and disrespect.

Folly's moral? Leave his wife excluded and he's a good son. Envision family intimacy, but not at the expense of his wife's dignity, he's a bad son.[38]

Sluggardly Folly

If naivete opens too quickly and quits too late, folly closes too quickly and quits too soon. Folly simply cannot imagine good coming from wisdom's invitation to change and grows sluggardly with wiser things[39] (Prov. 24:30; 26:16).

1) A sluggard wants good but won't do what securing good requires.

> The soul of the sluggard craves and gets nothing (Prov. 13:4; 21:25).
>
> The sluggard does not plow in the autumn; he will seek at harvest and have nothing (Prov. 20:4).

Like a person desiring harvest who won't plant when its time, is a fool who craves good relationships but neglects the wiser things good relationships are made of.

2) They'll say, "I'll do what it takes!" but won't finish what wise counselors commend.

> The sluggard buries his hand in the dish and will not even bring it back to his mouth (Prov. 19:24; 26:15).

"Look. I've buried my hand in the dish. See, I'm doing the work." Like one who gets up early, hunts game, but leaves the killed animal to rot (Prov. 12:27), folly says yes to wise counsel but quits soon after. Justifying itself, it says, "Well, if you only knew what threatens me, you'd see how easy you have it and how wrong you are to ask me to follow through" (Prov. 22:13; 26:13).

By choosing unnecessarily harder paths and feeling righteous about it, sluggards make it painful and costly to love them (Prov. 10:26; 15:19).

3) Consequently, folly sometimes chooses silent treatments
Anger is vented *about* you, not *to* you.

> The one who conceals hatred has lying lips, and whoever utters slander is a fool (Prov. 10:18).

A silent treatment "conceals" displeasure, withholds delight, withdraws curiosity, and prioritizes unspoken condemnation. It only proves our point if the loved one doesn't figure out their sin by our punishing silence. "See, I was right about you!"

It narrates a lying or conjectured story to selective friends at Bible study, work, or to other family members. How longsuffering folly has been. How righteous, how loving.

Consider a girl, fourteen, who moves to her dad's house. Her local paper features her playing the flute. The caption states she's from the city in which her dad lives.

Seeing the caption, relatives on her mom's side withdraw their love. How could she tell the reporter she's from her dad's town, not theirs? Instead of celebrating, they create environments of silence, waiting punishingly for the girl to confess her disrespect.

They've no idea the reporter didn't ask but assumed her residence because of the new high school she attends. She's just a kid grateful for a happy moment, amid the hardship of changing schools. She cries each night over friends and family she had to leave because the recurring adult choices of divorce are swamping her little boat. But this never occurs to them.

"Foolishness wants to be adored and obeyed."[40] Folly will covet, compete with, or correct our joy, but it won't celebrate unless our accomplishments, opinions, conversations, or experiences honor it.

One Greater than Solomon Has Come

To glimpse how Jesus heals our foolish hearts, let's compare how Jesus relates to the woman at the well with how Jesus relates to a lawyer inquiring about eternal life (Luke 10:25-37):

The lawyer raises a question.

In response, Jesus answers with a question.

"How do you read it?"

The lawyer answers by quoting the Bible.

Jesus responds with affirmation and quiet.

Unsettled by Jesus' quiet, the man tries to justify himself.

And there it is. What Jesus knew all along but we didn't. This isn't an authentic conversation. The lawyer is using it to preserve his own opinions and to have Jesus sanction them. In response, Jesus tells a story and then asks another question.

"Which one proved to be the neighbor?"

The lawyer answers.

Jesus responds with affirmation and more quiet.

At the well, Jesus spoke of wonder, the woman's past relationships, how God is Spirit and Jesus the promised one. What an intimate letter compared to the sparse email Jesus gives this man.

Wisdom approaches folly differently than naivete. With folly:

> *Wisdom considers not answering:* "Answer not a fool according to his folly, lest you be like him yourself. Answer a fool according to his folly, lest he be wise in his own eyes." (Prov. 26:4-5; Eccles. 3:7)

First, *wisely we slow down to discern ourselves.* Are we about to respond to folly with folly? If so, we must stop (lest you be like him yourself) (Luke 6:42).

Second, *wisely we slow down to discern others.* If folly interprets our sparse talk as cheering for it, we must answer (lest he be wise in his own eyes).

Third, with folly, *wisdom uses fewer words and more boundaries.*

> Do not speak in the hearing of a fool, for he will despise the good sense of your words (Prov. 23:9).

> Leave the presence of a fool, for there you do not meet words of knowledge (Prov. 14:7).

But how does the boundaried quiet of wisdom differ from the punishing silent treatments of folly?

- Notice that Jesus remains warmly present, relationally engaged, full of willing love.

- Jesus will never relate sparsely to the naive, or wounded, unlike the fool who corrects everyone no matter who they are.

- The foolish heart interprets others in the worst possible light on its own authority. Wisdom assumes another's best, amid wise counsel, choosing slowness to speak, quickness to listen and slowness to vent anger, so all persons are heard, known, and rightly discerned.

- Fool's boundaries are punishments that demand we stay foolish. Wise boundaries are acts of grace, freeing others from their slavish orbit around us, toward God again.

Fourth, why does Jesus use sparse talk and stories with a foolish heart?

First, the parable is a revealer. Everyone but a fool (or scoffer) will humble themselves and ask to be taught the meaning of the story (Mark 4:10-12).

Second, indirect speech moves toward the will in roundabout ways. A foolish heart shuts down direct confrontation but lingers longer when the finger pointing at it points first at an analogy or scene.

To a naive heart, Jesus' approach sounds mean. But folly complacently (Prov. 1:32) and willfully uses their own hands to tear wisdom down (Prov. 14:1). It creates unnecessary sorrows into the lives of those who've tried to love them (Prov. 10:1; 17:21). Disgrace awaits a fool (Prov. 3:35).

In this light, *Wisdom is willing to move on.*

Once, fools found Jesus offensive which made His disciples nervous (Matt. 15:12-14).

Jesus responded in two ways.

First, Jesus said, "Let them alone." Why? Because they are blind guides. They imagine themselves as seers but they ask no questions and pursue no learning from Jesus. Conversation with them isn't genuine but a way they use to manipulate others toward their own opinion and demand them to align to it.

Second, Jesus chose instead to prioritize time with open hearts. He turns to the crowds, "Hear and understand," He says. He answers honest questions His disciples ask.

Foolish Pharisees and scribes constantly hound Jesus. Folly can't rest if it doesn't have the last word.

But Jesus has a life to live and a ministry to fulfill. Jesus doesn't chase or constantly correct those who are offended by Him. Neither should we (Matt. 15:12-14).

Wise healing for a foolish heart requires winsome subversion, given us by His Spirit sustained in us by His grace.

Is there Hope for Foolish Hearts?
Yes!

> Fools, when will you be wise? (Ps. 94:8)

Repentant hearts answer.

> My wounds stink and fester because of my foolishness. (Ps. 38:5ff)

Perhaps someone you love is inviting you to see a blind spot hindering your relationship. You've deflected by pointing out their faults. They've responded by asking forgiveness for any true wrong they've done.

You growled and said, "I'm sorry that *you* ..." But what happened next, you didn't expect. For the first time in their lives, they're less naive with you. Instead of remaining quiet or saying "whatever," or "it's all good" or "you're right," they asked a question, commended what they could of your answer, let you know that they see things differently than you and said nothing more.

In response, you write an email growling a series of questions that aren't questions but insinuations and misinterpretations. For the first time in your life, your loved one does not answer your email. Or, after two or three days, they write:

> Thank you for emailing me. I long for a relationship where we can keep up together like this. But I see how your email begins, so I'm not going to read it. I love you. Let's talk instead.

Now you growl intensely (Eccles. 10:14). They respond with boundary.

> I love you. I'm not going to talk like this anymore, okay? It isolates us with no one who loves us nearby. What if we ask mutual friends who care about us both to listen next time, or a counselor or pastor that we both trust? I love you and want to learn a different way together.

You're furious. You try mirroring their wisdom; like a mockingbird, pirating phrases from the wisdom trying to reach you (Prov. 17:28). But your loved one keeps refusing the fight (Prov. 16:20).

You now stand at Rehoboam's crossroads.

"Thump your chest" your growling heart advises.

But wisdom gently subverts you:

Humble yourself
Listen to understand
Respond kindly
Enact a patient plan over time
Trust will deepen
The kingdom will flourish

Imagine if Rehoboam had chosen wisdom. It's true, he'd have lost foolish friends, who if given the choice of a wiser Rehoboam, would rather not have him at all. But his kingdom would have flourished. As it is, Rehoboam thumped the chest and risked becoming broken "beyond healing" (Prov. 29:1).

All the while, with heaving tears, the one trying to reach you prays for you, for the loss you're choosing, as she tries painfully to come out from under the condemning misrepresentations you've multiplied about her life. Wise friends hold your loved one and lament. "It could be so different," they say as they, too, pray for you.

Imagine you said:

> I know I'm wrong in ways I can't see. I don't even know how to begin or understand why you're relating to me this way. But I love you and want our relationship healed. I've been a fool and I'm so sorry.

Wisdom will respond with greater openness than folly can imagine. The grace voice of wisdom beckons you. "O fools, learn sense!" (Prov. 8:5).

This good sense is found in Jesus who will:

> Free you from interpreting others in the worst negative light (Prov. 11:12).
>
> Free you from twisted reasoning birthed out of that self-authoritative interpretation (Prov. 12:8).

Free you from pursuing life purposes that will leave you empty (Prov. 12:11).

Free you from the energy required to defend every perceived slight (Prov. 19:11).

Free you to offer wise instruction to others that waters them into life (Prov. 16:22).

Free you to feel full love within you in a way that folly never allowed (Prov. 19:8).

Free you from being ruled by anger, from turning every minnow into a whale (Prov. 19:11).

Free you to receive the teaching of the wise and name it wise (Prov. 23:9).

Free you from the blind spot of folly that others always saw plainly in you (Eccles. 10:3).

Free you finally to taste the joy and pleasure of wiser love with God, your family, friends (Prov. 15:21).

In our last chapter, we tasted the hope wisdom offers the naive.

Whoever is simple, let him turn in here!

Now we taste another grace-wonder. Wisdom invites us fools, too.

To him *who lacks sense* she says,
"Come, eat of my bread ... and live" (Prov. 9:4-6).

4

When We Scoff

You're a villain.
You're stealing parts of my soul ...[41]

Sunday mornings, I stroll smilingly to Riverside Church. An older couple walks their dogs. A woman jogs head-phoned in rhythm. A fit-bit man hurries stroller and baby.

Sometimes, a lone man walks toward me. No one else but us inch along this stretch of sidewalk. Whether he smiles, regardless of race, the closer he gets, the more I struggle to breathe.

I try to look safe and neighborly. As he passes, I angle my head to peer back over my shoulder. Will he continue or halt his stride? I'm surveilling him now.

Forty-five years ago, a stranger chased me down the sidewalk, my ten-year-old legs and lungs heaving into a corner grocery, where the man waited and waited and so did I.

That same year, a relative kept touching me where no relative should.

Twenty-nine years ago, a man on campus invited me to lunch after church. I fled his house of "back rubs."

No wonder the closely timed ski-masked prank in the midnight woods of college friendship curled me up into a ball.

Twenty years ago, I ran barefoot in my T-shirt toward a gang beating up a neighborhood kid. The gang's displeasure nightly surrounded our house, pounding walls, with my little ones asking, "What's that noise, Daddy?"

Sleep became nightmare a long while after that.

It's been years, I'm saying, but I find myself checking over my fifty-five-year-old shoulder when walking past a man on a sunlit morning.

Some habits bring out our memorized hurts, reveal our haunted past.

A sadder thought.

For somebody, I'm that man. They're walking and trying to look as safe and neighborly as possible. They're peering over their shoulder to see whether I've halted or walked on. We're both like deer alert and wide-eyed, trying to discern the footsteps of a hunter from those of a child.

Sadder still. Tame are the memories I'm describing. In this world, "there are wrongs done to innocence that scorch the mind."[42]

Becoming a Student of Wisdom

Proverbs opens with a glimpse into how sages teach their students (Prov. 1:1-7). We are not surprised that these sages describe the skill set of wisdom. They will learn discretion, prudence, wise dealing, wise insight and the riddles of the wise (Prov. 1:1-6).

Nor are we surprised that in this wisdom overview, sages establish wisdom's worldview for their students. "The fear of the LORD is the beginning of wisdom" (Prov. 1:7), which is to say, all of life is tethered to God and we live our lives knowing we are in God's world and all things are His.

But it might surprise us that once sage teachers introduce students to wisdom's skill set and worldview, their first step in this introductory class is to ask them to consider a case study about murder and theft.

First, the student hears how a person talks when finding joy in harming others.

Second, the student hears in contrast, how a wise father and mother talk about these misguided pleasures of a scoffer, who tear down neighbor love for fun.

"My son," the wise parents say, "Do not go with them" (Prov. 1:8-19).

Sage teachers begin their pedagogy of wisdom by introducing their students to what a scoffer craves on the menu of loves. How do we know what wisdom is? For a start, one must first learn how to discern a scoffer's talk and the dynamism of his misguided appeal to our happiness.

Anatomy of a Scoffer's Heart

Naive hearts rob tears. Foolish hearts steal ease and individuality. Scoffing hearts take our dignity. The time, choices and purposes of our lives are invaded and derailed here.

> *A scoffing heart takes advantage of the one who weeps, tears down the one who rejoices.*

"Scoffer is the name of the arrogant, haughty man who acts with arrogant pride" (Prov. 21:24). Relishing "vain words and lies" (Ps. 4:2), he loves violence, wrongdoing (Ps. 11:5; Prov. 17:5, 19), devouring others.

> You love evil more than good,
> and lying more than speaking what is right. Selah
> You love all words that devour,
> O deceitful tongue (Ps. 52:3-4).

Criminal cravers aren't "hurting people by accident. They use a gracious lip to disguise the dark weather within their heart; a fervent word like glistening glaze to masquerade the jagged edges of their cracked pottery (Prov. 26:23-25). They want to get better at their craft of breaking jaws just as you want to get better at art or music."[43]

Naivete feels it unloving to say this, but there are people in the world who declare harm a delight. Flannery O'Connor exposes this truth through a fictional serial killer she calls, "the misfit." If Jesus was who He said He was, grumbles the misfit, we should all leave off everything and follow Him. But since Jesus wasn't:

> it's nothing for you to do but enjoy the few minutes you got left the best way you can—by killing somebody or burning down his house or doing some other meanness to him. No pleasure but meanness.[44]

A scoffer isn't the bully in fifth grade, insecure and needing love, but a bully fully grown who loves causing fear. Such persons

> cannot sleep unless they have done wrong;
> they are robbed of sleep unless they have made someone to stumble (Prov. 4:16).

Like a brown recluse spider, scoffers hide in dark corners to poison you. But unlike the spider, the scoffer is looking to harm you. He'll travel miles into a city-wide protest. Unlike local people gathered with courage for peace, he'll foment violence, destroy neighborhoods, hurt people (Prov. 24:9; 29:8).

Two consequences squirm the naive heart.

1. We must take better care with sayings like, "do what you want." At best, these notions honor individual dignity. At

worst, we're saying "you do you" to persons giddy with iniquity.

Shouldn't our natural desires sometimes be denied? Like, what if your natural desire is to step on a baby?[45]

2. We must face the powerlessness of pursuing clarity and reason with a scoffer.

... a scoffer does not listen to rebuke (Prov. 13:1; Prov. 15:12).

The issue isn't that we used the wrong emoji, emailed a flawed sentence, spoke an unclear reason. A scoffing heart doesn't care about wisely placed emoji's, sentences, or reasons.

While a foolish critic laughs or rages to enslave your opinion to theirs, a scoffing critic cares nothing about your opinion.

Try to teach the naive, they'll laugh and divert you.
Teach the fool and they'll correct you.
Instruct a scoffer? They'll physically beat you.

Whoever corrects a scoffer gets himself abuse, and
he who reproves a wicked man incurs injury. Do not
reprove a scoffer, or he will hate you (Prov. 9:7-8).[46]

A scoffing client sends personal letters to his therapist's home address, making it plain, "I know where you and your family live."

The Tactics of a Scoffing Heart

Samson and Delilah picture the historical equivalent to fictional Snow White. Enemies pay Delilah to seduce Samson with promises of love, intimacy, and sex, in order to discover the secret vulnerability to his God-given strength (Judges 16:5).

Three times, Samson tests Delilah. Three times Delilah proves her intent to harm him.

Wisdom would say, "Samson, close the door. No matter how pretty or sexy, intelligent, or cozy. Harm crouches to devour you."

Delilah's words reveal a scoffer's relational tactics.

> How can you say, "I love you," when your heart is not with me? You have mocked me these three times and you have not told me where your great strength lies (Judges 16:15).

Samson had a wise hunch to test the situation. Delilah berates Samson's wise hunch narrating his wisdom as meanness and deceit (you've mocked me and told me lies); the worst accusation a naive heart can imagine.

Then, Delilah plays the victim, describing Samson's wise boundary as an indicator of his shallow love, falsely indicting him as a hypocrite ("How can you say 'I love you' when your heart is not with me"). Another accusation a naive heart cannot bear.

Delilah describes herself, not Samson. She is mean and heartless, not him.

But naive hearts hate being unenjoyed and narrated as unloving, even by a wicked heart.

To seal his naivete, a scoffer's final tactic, relentlessly steals quiet. Pressure escalates. Stress intensifies. In essence, Delilah says, "let go of wisdom. Remain naive toward me; imagine the love life we'd share together if you did, the deeper, truer person you'd be." Samson wearies.

> And when she pressed him hard with her words, day after day . . . his soul was vexed (v.16).

"She's right," crowded and bullied Samson says naively to himself. "I've not loved her well. I've held back my heart thinking she isn't safe. That was mean of me."

He lets wisdom's mirror go and looks instead to find himself within the bully's portrayal. The result? Naive Samson "told her all his heart" (Judges 16:15-17) and suffered for it.

Samson lost his eyes and his life.

Delilah got paid.

Wisdom's Way with the Scoffing Heart

Naive hearts need Jesus' wondrous invitation to the brought low places.

Foolish hearts need Jesus' winsome subversion.

But scoffing hearts will need Jesus' woeful confrontation.

Condemnation is ready for scoffers (Prov. 19:29).

The wise name a scoffer's tactics clearly, condemn them publicly, and remove them decisively through court. Encouraging a scoffer to be kind, follow policy and heed citation, will not work. We "have to go into protection mode, not helping mode."[47]

Drive out a scoffer, and strife will go out, and quarreling and abuse will cease (Prov. 22:10).

When a scoffer is punished, the simple becomes wise (Prov. 21:11; 19:25).

Hence, the scoffer depends upon the presence of the naive in order to flourish. When we refuse to bring criminal action and its technical legalities into accountable consequence, the naive give their hearts to those who'll craftily and happily crush them. A trail of pain follows as no one stands up to the scoffer.

For example:

- the scoffing parent or relative whom the rest of the family protects with secrets

- the scoffing employee whom management protects because of their high sales numbers
- the scoffing Christian leader whom the board protects because of celebrity persona or institutional reputation
- the scoffing politician whom an entire populace will excuse even in the name of God, because he upholds their policy interests.

Naivete can't imagine that God could meet them in their lowest places and bring them safely to the other side. "If we confront or lose this scoffing person, how can our business, church, country, or family survive?"

So, naivete entrusts itself to an untrustworthy person rather than to God's wisdom and care. Consequences follow.

> Trusting in a treacherous man in time of trouble is like a bad tooth or a foot that slips (Prov. 25:19).

The culture that protects a scoffing leader will begin to re-narrate, blame shift, pressure, and berate wiser family members, employees, or constituents. Wisdom begins to get punished. Scoffing gets protected. The scoffer no longer needs to do this himself. The culture now does it for him, "holding accountable" anyone wise who is unwilling to remain naive.

Unwise revenue, celebrity reputation, and institutional interests get preserved. But the cost pierces all involved with the new wincing normality of an unrelieved ache throbbing within the roots of all their mouths. The cavities worsen with no one to heal them.

One Greater than Solomon Has Come

Is there hope for a scoffing heart? Yes.

Jesus confronts scoffers in two direct ways.

(1) He says "no."
(2) He defends those scoffed at.

For example, Samaritans refuse Jesus. James and John want them dead in God's name.

(1) Jesus rebukes James and John strongly (Luke 9:51-55).
(2) Jesus doesn't stop heroizing Samaritans in His stories or as neighbors to be loved (Luke 10:33-37).

Or consider when Peter draws his sword in Gethsemane.

(1) "Put that away," Jesus says.
(2) Then, Jesus publicly shows mercy to the one Peter harmed.

If we are tempted to scoff, Jesus will look into our eyes, say "no," and defend the dignity of those we scoffed at.

"Isn't that mean of Jesus?" says the naive heart.

"No," we say. "It's wise of Him."

But how do we discern the difference between scoffers and those being tempted to scoff?

Simply put, those tempted to scoff yield to Jesus' correction. When Jesus said no, Peter, James, and John, each put down their killing quests and obeyed.

But what happens if a scoffer doesn't yield to Jesus' correction?

Holding Up the Mirror

Jesus "holds up a mirror" as it were.

Saul of Tarsus is physically jolted, smacked with pure light, knocked onto his backside, and sentenced to blindness for three days. Jesus does not subject the woman at the well, the lawyer who justifies himself, Peter or the sons of thunder to this level of confrontation.

Within this forceful consequence, Jesus exposes Saul with a question.

Saul,
Saul,
why?

Consider three more examples of how Jesus uses questions to hold up a mirror to scoffers.

1. The Jews picked up stones again to stone him. Jesus answered them:

   I have shown you many good works from the Father; for which of them are you going to stone me (John 10:31-32)?

2. The high priest scoffingly questions Jesus. Jesus answers:

   I have spoken openly to the world. I have always taught in synagogues and in the temple, where all Jews come together. I have said nothing in secret. Why do you ask me? Ask those who have heard me what I said to them; they know what I said. (John 18:20-21).

At this, "one of the officers standing by struck Jesus with his hand" (v. 22).

3. Notice how Jesus again uses a question as a mirror:

   If what I said is wrong, bear witness about the wrong; but if what I said is right, why do you strike me (John 18:23)?

In each case, the One Greater than Solomon, holds up two contradictory actions to the scoffer, and then exposes these contradictions with a question that requires the scoffer to look truthfully at the criminality he is choosing.

The wise good Jesus gives them	The scoffing they choose in response
I have shown you many good works from the Father ...	For which of them are you going to stone me?
I have spoken openly to the world. I have always taught in synagogues and in the temple, where all Jews come together. I have said nothing in secret ...	Why do you ask me?
If what I said is wrong, bear witness about the wrong; but if what I said is right ...	Why do you strike me?

Finding Hope

Is there hope for a scoffer? Yes. Jesus takes the curse of our scoffing upon Himself. He bears the brunt of our delight in meanness. He pays the curse of it to free us from it.

For example, from a cross adjacent to Jesus, a criminal watches the religious leaders, soldiers, and a fellow criminal scoff at Jesus. They delight in Jesus' agony, while Jesus the wise lover beseeches their forgiveness from the Father (Luke 23:35-39). Until now, all his life this watching criminal would have joined in. By scoffing they're speaking his native language. But something's happening. He can't stomach it anymore. The wiser grace of God in Christ is breaking through. For the first time in his life, this criminal on a cross next to Jesus looks upon the ugliness of this scoffing scene as if in a mirror. He then takes three actions any scoffer must take to have any hope of rescue.

1. Instead of scoffingly narrating Jesus and Jesus' wisdom, the criminal publicly and forcefully rebukes this false narration. (The other rebuked him)

2. Instead of shifting blame, the criminal confesses the wise justice of his own consequences and defends the wise one

as innocent. (We are receiving the due reward for our deeds. This man has done nothing wrong)

3. Rather than delighting in the pleasure of scoffing, the criminal newly craves the wiser way and love of Jesus, and humbles himself (Remember me). To be thought well of by the wise is something a scoffing heart cares nothing about. This once-scoffing man is being changed by the grace of God right before our eyes.

Jesus' turns his bloodied face justly toward the criminal.

Jesus' mercy looks into criminal eyes.

Then come the grace words.

"Today," says the One Greater than Solomon, "You will be with me in paradise."

Even a scoffer who looks to the cross of Christ can be changed.

Humbled by such undeserved love, forgiven scoffers like Saul of Tarsus can't stop talking about this grace of God in Christ. They appeal to you with hope. If God could save the worst of scoffers like me, they'll say, imagine how able He is to rescue you (1 Tim. 1:12-17).

What if? Putting it All Together

Step back now. Retrace the thread of our opening chapters in this book. Consider how differently Jesus relates to the naive, the fool, and the scoffer.

In this light, I have a "what if?" question for you.

What if when Jesus began His earthly ministry He spoke with plain instruction, wonder, and invitation, because He assumed each listener either naive or wise till proven otherwise?

What if after a while, Jesus discerned scribes, Pharisees and others, as growling lions, baring teeth? They asked questions not to learn by honest talk, but to justify and preserve their own opinions. Discerning this, Jesus wisely shifted to a barrage of parables (Mark 4:11).

I'm saying, *What if* Jesus gradually shifted from the plain talk of wondrous invitation to the parabolic riddles of winsome subversion because the One Greater than Solomon was now accounting for foolish hearts growling at Him within the crowds?

Could this explain the surprise we have when reading the later chapters of Jesus' life for the first time? Take the gospel of Matthew. Jesus begins with "blessed are," and plain teaching. Then moves to parables, "the kingdom of heaven is like." Occasionally, a third kind of speech peeks through.

> Woe to you (Matt. 11:20-24; 18:7)!

To this point such woeful speech remains highly unusual and rare when listening to Jesus. Almost no one hears it. But after nearly three years into his ministry, in Matthew 23, Jesus shocks anyone accustomed to listening to Him the previous two. He takes up the prophetic mantle.

> Woe to you!
> Woe to you!
> Woe to you!
> Woe to you!
> Woe to you!
> Woe to you!
> Woe to you!

What if nearing the end of His public ministry, Jesus turns to woeful condemnation because those listening now include scoffers, and Jesus knows it? They aren't just naive or foolish listeners but include hypocrites scheming in the name of God to murder Jesus. These woes not only denounce the scoffer with strength but include Jesus' defense of those scoffed at (Matt 23:1ff).

What if we're learning from Jesus, to discern the heart in front of us and to wisely relate accordingly?

Jesus didn't treat someone as a scoffer because they differed with Him, made a mistake or sinned. Jesus never pronounced woe upon the woman at the well, nor Zacchaeus, nor any of Jesus' students, nor Samaritans, nor the centurion. Even Peter, who heard "Get behind me, Satan," did not hear the prophetic woe pronounced against him.

Moreover, Jesus bore with scribes and Pharisees nearly three years before donning the prophetic mantle. "Woe to you" wasn't Jesus' default mode of speaking.

We foolish hearts must ask ourselves, "Why do I default to pronouncing woe on others" when Jesus clearly didn't? Why do I woefully confront women at the well, tax collectors in trees, and earnest disciples tempted to wrong, when Jesus doesn't?

In contrast, we naive hearts must grapple with Jesus, who, with time and discernment, will eventually pronounce woe. A naive heart must ask why it has no category for this when Jesus clearly does.

What if we're learning too, to discern the heart we bring within us. Perhaps we're beginning to understand, maybe for the first time, why it is Jesus relates to us the way He does and why His way with us now might differ from an earlier season in our lives or from His current way with a friend?

And now a harder word. We scoffing hearts must wake up to the Jesus we are dealing with.

Jesus is no wilting Samson. He sees through the hag's threefold knock at the door and shuts it. He exposes the treachery for all to see and puts an end to it.

Not only is Jesus king, but Jesus discerns you.

> A king who sits on the throne of judgment
> winnows all evil with his eyes (Prov. 20:8).

He will say no to you and defend those you scoff at. He will knock you off your horse if need be.

And now dear wounded heart, dear naive heart, dear earnest, and wise heart, I'm not speaking to you. I speak now to the scoffer alone.

Dear scoffing heart, you're naked and known before Him.
It's time to unhide.
The wise one has found you out.

> A wise king winnows the wicked
> and drives the wheel over them (Prov. 20:26).

Jesus is the true and wise king. And aren't all His "woes to you" still grace-words? He is, after all, still speaking to you.

He tried to invite you to wonder. He tried to subvert you winsomely. Now He is knocking you off your horse with woeful condemnation. What grace! Repentance is still possible. Forgiveness and new life still yours to receive.

I'm saying, the prophetic woes of King Jesus aren't the most frightful things.

The most frightful thing, oh scoffing heart, is not Jesus' woe but His silence. Would that He would knock you off your horse and blind you rather than no longer speak to you.

> When he was accused by the chief priests and elders, [Jesus] gave no answer.
> Then Pilate said to him, "Do you not hear how many things they testify against you?"
> But [Jesus] gave him no answer (Matt. 27:12-14).

No more invitations to Jesus' wonder.

> Herod was very glad to see Jesus; for a long time he had wanted to see him because he had heard about him and was hoping

to see some miracle performed by him. So he kept asking him questions, but Jesus did not answer him (Luke 23:8-11, CSB).

No more of Jesus' subversive parables.

No more of Jesus' woe to you.

Behold the active and righteous silence of the Son of God bearing witness amid the injustices of your making.

Every victim of yours He stands with and defends.

Take heed. Could these last lingering moments of His silence even now retain mercy enough to recover you?

It's not too late.

It's not too late.

It's ...

5

When We're Crushed in Spirit

*What if what you do to survive
kills the things you love?*[48]

A dear woman scorched our Associate Pastor with an email. He responded.

> Zack and I hate the thought of hurting you.
> I'd like to listen. May we meet?

He hit "send," and she sped another email. Then a third arrived. This time from her husband. Despite compassionate invitation, intensity escalated.

So, I went to this cherished family's home. The husband stepped onto the porch, muscles tensed like he could punch me. Sadly, my first reaction intensified too. Then I thought, "What kind of fool are you, Zack? Standing on the porch of a family you love, holding the Bible and, what, you're going to fight?"

Dear reader, old folly dies hard. It creeps into you when you least expect it. But though it rears its wicked head and it crushes you to see it, you needn't wait to cut it off. You aren't that old fool anymore. One greater than Solomon has paid for you. He stands there with you ready to empower you.

So, I relax, remembering who this man is, who I am, and whose we are.

His wife pushes through the door, her heart like a hornet's nest someone kicked. Her words fly out like a powerfully winged platoon, stinging with force, until their dear son with special needs surprises us by stepping out the door onto the porch.

"Pastor Zack! You're at my home!"

"Yes," I say, stumbling into a smile.

"I have to brush my teeth," he says. "What are you doing?"

"I'm visiting your family."

He reaches to give me the best of hugs and I offer my best in return.

"See you at church!" he says smiling.

"I'd love that," I say.

As he goes, the hornets relent. Tears flow. I sit with her, her husband standing like a marine.

"It's so hard wherever we go," she cries. "They stare. They make comments. They talk loud to my son or down to him. Grocery stores, schools, *churches*. I just thought this church was different."

As she talks, I learn that a house group at our church closed entrance to a special needs family. This painful exclusion against that other family broke this one's heart.

I'd need to visit that other pained family and we'd equip that house group, but by God's grace both families remained in our church, which often isn't how a story like this turns out.

Sometimes, what growls at you isn't a reactive fool or a scoffer, but a crushed soul.

We need wisdom to discern the difference, lest we mistakenly treat a broken heart like a foolish one.

Wounds Tempt Us with Unwise Remedies

Why might a wounded heart fling itself into a fury?

One reason is that wounds tempt us to scoff. "Beware, lest wrath *entice you* into scoffing" (Job. 38:18).[49]

When pained, we're tempted to inflict the same injustices we once protested, the same pains we once lamented.

> A poor man who oppresses the poor is a beating rain that leaves no food (Prov. 28:3).

This poor man afflicts those whose pain he most understands.

But wounds tempt us to folly, too. Bereft of her children, Job's wife helplessly watches her husband's agony. They both endure mental and physical anguish with no ability to lay weeping within each other's arms.

"Do you still hold fast your integrity?" she asks. "Curse God and die" (Job 2:9).

Job does not say, "You foolish woman," but "You speak *as one of the foolish women would speak*" (v. 10). Amid the howl of her grief her broken heart gives way to folly's growl.

A broken heart is like a wasp in your house. It gets lost inside your window. It keeps flicking itself against the glass. It flutters and buzzes not to hurt you but to escape you.

But make no mistake. Try helping it home and that wasp will sting you.

And no wonder, considering how others respond when they see our wasp-like struggles up close.

- The naive leave us, watch a show, read the Bible, tell us it'll all work out.

- Foolish helpers fluster about, roll up a magazine and smack us.

- Scoffers delight in watching our struggle. They find ways to intensify our misery.
- Broken apart helpers collapse into a heap or fling themselves to inflict one of these other three strategies upon you.

A *double wound* emerges.

First, Job and his wife are sunk deep into the floodwaters of relational, vocational, economic, bodily, and spiritual devastation.

Second, Job's friends open their mouths to help and nearly drown them.[50]

Perhaps you can now see why the wise deem suffering of the soul more brutal than bodily suffering.

> A man's spirit will endure sickness, but a crushed spirit who can bear (Prov. 18:14)?

C.S. Lewis describes this burden.

> Mental pain is less dramatic than physical pain, but it is more common and also more hard to bear ... it is easier to say, "My tooth is aching" than to say, "My heart is broken."[51]

Healing our Relational Hallucinations

Broken hearts cause us to hallucinate—to imagine ghosts when none are there.

Consider a drawing of Santa offering a boy a teddy bear. Yet, the boy looks haunted rather than happy. The caption explains.

> Unwisely, Santa offered a teddy bear to James, unaware that he'd been mauled by a grizzly earlier that year.[52]

Sometimes what appears to us as a wasp on our window is a ladybug. Our crushed spirit imagines a winged stinger ready to puncture our skin when what crawls toward us is a gentle beauty.

In our wiser moments we all know that wasps and ladybugs are both insects, that one will sting you and the other won't. But when sinned against, we can lose this ability and are prone to treat both bugs alike.

So with people. Our wounds prejudge the smiling person in our present as no different than the hurtful person in our past. Like when the woman at the well said, "How is it that you, a Jew, ask for a drink from me, a woman of Samaria?" (John 4:9). Jesus looked like pain but wasn't.

When I see an envelope with "pastor" written on it, my body jitters, and my heart rate rises. Perhaps the envelope has a ladybug within it, but everything in me readies for the wasp that will fly out to sting me once I open it.

One Sunday afternoon a husband telephoned and told me I'd spoken negatively about a song in the morning sermon.

"My wife led worship last week, remember?"

"Yes," I said.

"*Turn Your Eyes Upon Jesus* was one of the songs," he replied.

My heart sank.

"If you're going to call out a worship volunteer publicly like that," he said, "we just don't think we can go to this church anymore and it's killing us because we love this church."

I was stunned. I'd commended the song, enjoyed it, asked us to consider how one specific lyric could be viewed differently, and felt nothing but gratitude and love for our worship leader.

"If I ever did something like that, called you out like that, you'd be right to feel outraged and wise to leave. I'm so sorry. May I come over?"

Once we saw each other, the bubble of imagined frowns popped. We recognized each other within the gracious light of our own positive story together rather than the painful shadows of previous interactions with others.

A dear friend once remarked.

> Why can my past become so suddenly present to me? My wounds are like the side mirror on my car saying, "Be careful, the things behind you are closer than they appear."

How can a broken heart find healing amid this swirl of painful enticements, double wounds, and "relational hallucinations?" Sage teachers show us how.

First, we need to experience the gentle talk of the wise.

> A gentle tongue is a tree of life,
> but perverseness in it breaks the spirit (Prov. 15:4).

> Gracious words are like a honeycomb, sweetness to
> the soul and health to the body (Prov. 16:24).

The first time a wiser friend invites us to a harder conversation, we brace ourselves body and soul for sword-thrust talk, but the sword thrusts never come. Healing does.

> There is one whose rash words are like sword thrusts,
> but the tongue of the wise brings healing (Prov. 12:18).

Gradually, conversation upon conversation, this gentler way of the wise helps our body and soul rest rather than constantly scrambling vigilant into high alert.

Second, wisdom's gentler talk gradually enables us to recover our ability to tell the difference between a pain clothed with true friendship and the pain an enemy uses to harm us. For a while, we'd lost this ability and counted all pains synonymous with harm.

> Faithful are the wounds of a friend; profuse are the kisses of an enemy. (Prov. 27:6)

Consequently, the first few times we encounter conflict with a wiser lover, rather than the growly heart of a fool, we wonder what kind of confusing beauty this is.

We cried, and instead of robbing our tears, they validated them.

We disagreed, but they didn't rob our individuality; they grew curious.

We were vulnerable, and instead of robbing us of our dignity, they upheld it.

We were afraid, but they didn't rob our story; they honored it.

Yes, the conversation was hard. Hurt was real. But no one manipulated or withdrew love (Prov. 27:5). We both came away strengthened, not weakened, as if God rather than our wounds define us (Prov. 20:30).

Anatomy of a Crushed Spirit

Why is so much care required for us to heal?

Because a broken heart is like a walnut set between metal teeth and cracked open. We break into bits and get devoured.

> By sorrow of heart the spirit is crushed (Prov. 15:13).

Wise teachers sketch three primary causes of sorrow.

- *Headaches:* Our worried thoughts about ends not meeting, solutions not working, deadlines not helping. "Anxiety in a man's heart weighs him down" (Prov. 12:25).

- *Heartaches:* Our loss of people or things hoped for. "Hope deferred makes the heart sick" (Prov. 13:12).

- *Bodyaches:* Our physical sicknesses and discomforts along with the ways others have misused our bodies.[53]

Sometimes seasons intensify our sorrows by means of death or war, tearing away or weeping (Eccles. 3:1-8).

At other times, circumstances wound us, like having a fool for a boss at work, an alcoholic in charge of our care (Prov. 26:10), or someone with power leveraging our vulnerability (Prov. 22:22).

Sometimes we even cause our own wounds (Prov. 23:29).

Four kinds of a broken heart result:

- Newly broken
- Broken apart
- Broken open
- Flashback broken

Newly broken, we speak with wild honesty like a Psalmist and groan like Job in our distresses. People weep with us because weeping is the wisest thing we can do together.

Then, after a long, appropriate while, our brokenness grows older, and we must choose over and again, one of two diverging paths.[54]

On one path, we break apart. We get stuck in our story of pain as if we are Humpty Dumpty, and no one can put us back together again. The words, "If you only knew what I've gone through," so vital when newly broken, become the story we're still telling years later as if nothing else is truer about us.

When broken apart, we either over-weep or under-weep for others. When another rejoices, our pain escalates and we isolate ourselves. How can I celebrate the birth of her child when losing mine or when womb-barren?

We break apart when we habitually forego wiser healing, and choose naive, foolish, or scoffing medicines instead. If not careful, over time we become wounded harmers—inflicting hurt when someone celebrates.

In many a home there is a raw, red wound, and the healing of that wound seems very far away.[55]

But when by His grace, we break open, "the dross of hard experience can be transformed into the gold of wisdom."[56] After our newly broken seasons, we gradually learn again or for the very first time, to truly weep with those who weep and to experience the surprising goodness of rejoicing with those who rejoice. We become wounded healers.[57]

Even a wounded healer can be flashback broken.

When I stood on the porch, it became obvious that my friends were flashback broken, rather than normatively foolish. All it took was for their son to step out onto the porch and every truer good gathered us up and broke the hallucination.

A Community of Healing

So how do we break open rather than apart?

When Saul of Tarsus converted to Jesus, "They were all afraid of him for they did not believe that he was a disciple" (Acts 9:26-27). Saul had stung people. Their hesitance was wise.

"Lord," says Ananias, "I have heard from many about this man, how much evil he has done" (Acts 9:13).

In time, notice how they broke open with Saul.

- They needed "a faithful envoy" (Prov. 13:17), not a solo or manipulative messenger. Ananias and Barnabas were wise and trusted friends, along with wiser others who gradually witnessed Paul's changes first hand.
- They also needed time. Nothing forced, demanded, or pushed. Repentant Saul understood this.
- They needed an intervening empowerment from God in the context of a community of prayer (which in this extreme case included a supernatural vision).

"Breaking open," takes multi-layered help, wiser hearts and time, because when our hearts are crushed our "bones are troubled" (Ps. 6:2) too. They dry up (Prov. 17:22).

When I walk down the Sunday morning sidewalk and a stranger walks my way, it isn't just my soul that trembles, but my body. It must have been so for those who'd experienced Saul's scoffing damage first-hand. Wisdom mends our hearts and "refreshes the bones" (Prov. 15:30; 3:8).[58]

I've written elsewhere about embodied anxiety,[59] discerning those who sin against us[60] and what to do if the wounds in our lives are our own fault.[61] But for now, it is enough to observe that:

Newly broken, it was wise, body and soul, not to trust Saul of Tarsus.

And yet, it was wisdom, embodied and souled, that gradually broke open such trust.

One Greater Than Solomon

On the road to Emmaus (Luke 24), we who are crushed in spirit glimpse how the One Greater than Solomon disciples our wounds and brings healing to our bones.

1. In your pain, Jesus Gently Draws Near

> While they were talking and discussing together, Jesus himself drew near and went with them. But their eyes were kept from recognizing him (vv. 15-16).

Jesus doesn't 'start with Jesus' but with their plight. He travels with them as a quiet human rather than a verbal Savior.

2. Jesus Asks Gentle Questions

> And he said to them, "What is this conversation that you are holding with each other as you walk?" … And he said to them, "What things?" (vv. 17-19).

Jesus knows what pains them, yet He invites and asks rather than asserts and tells.

3. Jesus is Patient and Listens

> And they said to him ... (vv. 19-24).

Now for six verses, they speak, and Jesus doesn't.

4. Jesus Invites them to Consider their Wounds within the Biblical Story of His Wounds

> And he said to them, "O foolish ones, and slow of heart to believe ... Was it not necessary that the Christ should suffer?" ... And beginning with Moses and all the Prophets, he interpreted to them in all the Scriptures the things concerning himself (vv. 25-27).

Jesus relocates their experience within the biblical story of "the Christ." They look first at the biblical story together. Rather than having them look directly at Him, Jesus speaks in the third person.

Once relocated within the biblical story of His wounds, Jesus then says, "foolish ones," so gently, with love, that their hearts burn warmly, and they desire more, not less, of His presence. He is not saying "Woe" to scoffers but warning the wounded whom He loves that folly tempts them to break apart rather than open.

5. Jesus Provides Relational Time Without Relational Demands

> So they drew near to the village to which they were going. He acted as if he were going farther, but they urged him strongly, saying, "Stay with us" ... So he went in to stay with them (vv. 28-29).

Jesus doesn't demand their immediate understanding. He will draw nearer or farther according to their request. He is willing to "call it a night," move on and let them be.

6. *They Experience Epiphany While Experiencing Jesus' Consistent Way of Being*

> When he was at table with them, he took the bread and blessed and broke it and gave it to them. And their eyes were opened, and they recognized him (vv. 30-31).

Within this relational context of quiet presence, gentle questions, patient listening, and locating their wounds within the larger biblical story of the Christ, with room and no demand upon their time, it is startling to realize that it is their contact with Jesus' way of life that finally opens their eyes. They've seen Jesus break bread many times, but this time the lights turn on.

7. *They Experience the Scriptures Again in the Context of Felt Intimacy and the Primacy of Jesus*

> They said to each other, "Did not our hearts burn within us while he talked to us on the road, while he opened to us the Scriptures?" They rose that same hour ... found those gathered together ... told what happened ... (vv. 32-35).

When this conversation about their pain began, all their verbs were past tense. All they saw was wreckage. What happened in the past informed every step they took and fueled their initial frustration with Jesus' questions. But now! What pains them is seen through the light of Jesus' purpose back then, His renewing presence now, and future with Him that awaits them.[62]

Basking together, they resist the folly that tempted them. They choose wiser love, by moving toward wise community, sharing their hearts, and looking directly now at the One who made Himself known in their sorrows.

When the cares of my heart are many,
your consolations cheer my soul (Ps. 94:19).

Naive but Wounded

On the porch above we saw how wounds mask as folly. Naivete can intensify from wounds too.

In his *Letters to a Young Poet*, Rilke observes naive young lovers who impatiently "fling" themselves at each other. They shatter their solitude and call it love.[63]

Parents and mentors try to wisen these lovers by inviting them to cost-counting, discretion, and what it might mean to grow wiser with their wonder. "Healthier love," these mentors say, "consists in this: that two solitudes protect and border and salute each other."[64] Rather than collide and enmesh, guard your heart and the other, "for from it flow the springs of life" (Prov. 4:23).

But if one of these young lovers was raised in a home of divorce, a wound from abandonment can throb within. An invisible haste driving them slavishly to prove worthy enough not to be left again. Their way of love wears each of them out. They speak of their great love but are regularly tired, worn down, anxious.

The parents who see the anxious fatigue young love creates, try to intervene by "cost counting" and "prudence" and "discretion." If the parents feel unheard, they are tempted to foolishly withhold love from these young lovers or to naively shower their 'broken apart' loves with praise.

But because, in this case, these young lovers are not only naive, but wounded, they will need prudence, yes, but also consolation. Wisdom would lead these parents to draw near, not as a verbal savior, or neglectful cheerleader, but as a quiet human; to spend time asking questions of things the parent already knows so as to listen, learn, and be with them.

And after a while, if these parents speak from the Bible as a means to help their young lovers, the parents will speak more about Jesus and His wounds, as if the parents and the youth are both located and grace-needy within this same marvelous story.

And when the parents don't demand relational time but linger or leave according to what the youth can handle, it frees their youth to say, "don't go."

And then, to the great surprise of these parents at the end of this long road, late into the evening of their relationship, some small persistent way of their being in the world, such as how the parent always broke bread and gave it to others, will pour grace-light into memory, and wise insight into the present. Together, they'll eat with their hearts warming within them.

And perhaps in that moment, the parent, not just the child, will experience how Jesus has always drawn near to mentor and console us amid our wounded driveness and naive loves.

Jesus begins quiet and present as Job's friends did. But from there, Jesus goes on to do what Job's friends could not imagine and had no wisdom for. They thought Job a fool when in truth Job's heart was broken. They applied the wrong medicine having misdiagnosed the ailment. But the One Greater than Solomon is the true and great physician. He knows what troubles us. He is the healing our trouble calls for.

His Treasure Within

Where does this leave us but with God who heals the brokenhearted (Ps. 147:3).

Jesus declares "Woe" upon the scoffers who bruise you (Matt. 11:20-24).

Then, Jesus turns feelingly toward you, and giving thanks for the Father's love for you, He calls to your broken heart.

Come to me, all who labor and are heavy laden, and I will give you rest ... learn from me, for I am gentle and lowly in heart, and you will find rest for your souls (Matt. 11:28-30).

We are broken yes.
But by the grace of God in Jesus
with tears and time,
nearness and bandages,
Jesus has gently placed our wounds within the story of His,
and to our surprise, we're finding ourselves risking again,
moving awkwardly toward a community of
    healing relationships, which gradually
replace our wounded hallucinations with wiser imaginations,
because by the grace of God,
One Greater than Solomon has come.
We're breaking open,
and the wise treasure you're beginning to see in us,
is Him.

6

The Menu of Loves

*I believe in God and the whole business, but I love
women best, music and science next, whiskey next, God
fourth, and my fellowman hardly at all.
Generally, I do as I please.*[65]

Imagine a server provides you a menu.

If you say, "I'd like an entree, an à la carte and a drink, please," the server will necessarily respond, "Which entree, à la carte item, and drink would you like?"

Now imagine the menu provided is a menu of loves.

If you say, "I'd like an order of love, please," the server will likewise need to ask you a further question. "Which kind of love would you like? I can offer you naive love, foolish love, scoffing love, or broken-apart love. Our special tonight is wise love."

Offer wisdom or naivete to our naive hearts, and we'll choose naivete over wisdom because we've a craving for naive people, places, and things.

Set folly and wisdom on the table and invite our foolish hearts to choose whichever one delights our hearts, and we'll leave wisdom untasted because we have a hankering for foolish people, places, and things.

Love decides in favor of a delight. Love relishes something, then reaches for it. Love says of a person, place, thing, or idea "it is good that you exist! How wonderful you are."[66]

So, when we savor naive, foolish, scoffing or broken apart things, we say, "It is good that you exist!" We say to what damages us, "How tasty you are!"

Songwriter Ryan Tedder puts words to this.

> I feel something so right
> Doing the wrong thing
> And I feel something so wrong
> Doing the right thing ...
> Everything that kills me makes me feel alive.[67]

You've experienced this menu of loves in subtle ways.

A bridesmaid's speech platforms herself. She loves the bride but in that moment she loves naivete more.

A dad with talented children covets, corrects, or competes with them but rarely cheers them unless they orbit him. The dad loves his kids, but he loves folly more.

So, at the beginning of our human story, the serpent provides Adam and Eve a menu of different loves. He devilishly sets the tree groves of God's abundant provision in contrast to the one tree God prohibited. He invites them to place their order.

> When the woman saw that the tree was good ... a delight to the eyes ... to be *desired to make one wise*, she took of its fruit and ate, and she also gave some to her husband who was with her, and he ate (Gen. 3:6).

Jesus reveals this same ancient menu of loves by observing how we too repeat this mistake from Eden. Jesus says, we "*love darkness more than light*" (John 3:19, NLT).

1. *We are capable of loving unlovely things* (we love darkness).

2. *We can dislike or hate lovely things* (more than light).

3. *When we do love a good thing, we sometimes love it badly.*

We witness the outworking of this love for darkness more than light, when a religious man asks Jesus about eternal life with God.

"One thing you lack," Jesus says. "Sell what you have. Give to the poor. Do life with me" (Luke 18:18-23, my paraphrase). The man declines and walks away sad.

Jesus' question didn't challenge the man's worldview regarding "the search." "What should I do to inherit eternal life?" is a good question.

Nor did Jesus challenge the man's skill set regarding "the knack." "I've obeyed all these commandments since I was young," the man says, and Jesus accepts this.

The problem arises when Jesus hands the man a menu of loves, an X-ray revealing what captures the man's heart. With wisdom and un-wisdom offered to him, the man lets go of what he ought to relish (Jesus) and reaches for a good thing, badly (money).

The man was an exemplary believer, a skilled leader, but an unwise lover.[68]

Jesus often frames the lives of fine believers and skilled leaders through the lens of the unwise loves animating their hearts.

> They <u>love</u> to stand and pray in the synagogues and at the street corners, that they may be seen by others (Matt. 6:5).

> No one can serve two masters, for either he will <u>hate</u> the one and <u>love</u> the other, or he will be <u>devoted</u> to the one and <u>despise</u> the other (Matt. 6:24).

> Beware of the scribes, who <u>like</u> to walk around in long robes, and <u>love</u> greetings in the marketplaces and the best seats in the synagogues and the places of honor at feasts (Luke 20:46).

The earliest Christians learned this way of seeing the world through its loves. When Demas left the faith, they saw it as a problem of love, not just belief.

> Demas, <u>in love</u> with this present world, has deserted me (2 Tim. 4:10).

The relational pain Demas causes and the faith crisis Demas experiences arise because of what Demas loves.

A Startling Realization

"Hold on!" someone objects. "This menu stuff is too complicated. Just love from the heart and all will be well."

"No," says wisdom. "All won't be well."

"Why not?" we protest. "Our hearts are genuine!"

"Yes," the sages say. "Of that, we have no doubt."

"But I'm authentic," we say.

"Yes," they say. "Completely."

Hearing that, you and I stare at each other blankly.

So a sage steps closer and speaks kindly to us.

"Every heart needs a weather report. Is this true?"

We shrug our shoulders.

So, another steps forward and provides us wisdom phrases on worn parchment to read. We open it. It describes various conditions of heart.

> A heart can be broken (Ps. 51:17), faint (Job 23:16; Ps. 61:2), failing (Ps. 73:26), anxious (Prov. 12:25), sick (Prov. 13:12), bitter (Prov. 14:10), aching (Prov. 14:13), crushed (Prov. 15:13), heavy (Prov. 25:20), desirous (Job 17:11; Ps. 20:4), trembling (Job. 37:1), afflicted (Ps. 10:17), sorrowing (Ps. 13:2), stubborn

(Ps. 81:12), unfeeling (Ps. 119:70), wily (Prov. 7:10), crooked (Prov. 11:20), proud (Prov. 21:4), restless (Eccles. 2:23), madness (Eccles. 9:3), hardened (Job 41:24), tranquil (Prov. 14:30), glad, cheerful (Prov. 15:13, 15), intelligent (Prov. 18:15), merry (Eccles. 9:7), thrilled (Song 5:4) clean, pure (Ps. 51:10, 73:13), steadfast (Ps. 78:37), upright (Ps. 78:72), steady, firm, made whole (Ps. 119:10), perverse, arrogant (Ps. 101:4-5), stricken (Ps. 102:4, 109:22), godless (Job 36:13).

"OK," we say. "Yes. Each heart has its own weather."

"Good," she says. "Now, I ask you, is a proud heart genuine?"

You and I say, "Huh?"

"Whether arrogant or sorrowing, upright or perverse," she says, "each heart, true to itself, offers what is authentic to it, yes?"

She sees our blank stares. So she quotes the master.

"If a tree is good, its fruit will be good. If a tree is bad, its fruit will be bad" (Matt. 12:33, NLT).

She's speaking slowly but earnestly.

"When you offer your authentic heart," she continues, "you offer fruit from the kind of tree you are, words and actions from the condition of heart you possess" (Luke 6:45).

We don't get it at first but sages don't mind our awkward silence. Gradually, we catch on.

A naive heart when true to itself offers naivete authentically to the one it loves. A foolish heart when genuine will in the name of love, offer folly genuinely.

Pause here. Squint if you need to. Shift the angle in your seat. A glimpse of forgotten wisdom is about to pass right in front of us. Are you ready?

Most of us think difficulties with love stem from a *damaging incongruence,* what the wise call, a "double heart" (Ps. 12:2), or a "double mind" (James 1:8). What we call "hypocrisy."

We pretend not to love when we do (Prov. 27:5), or
to love when we don't (Ps. 55:21).

To remedy this hypocrisy, we say, "just love authentically from the heart."

The wise agree, but they add that being true to our hearts can equally sabotage our relationships. This kind of *damaging congruence* explains why an adult might say of her parents or spouse, "They didn't love me," while a sage counselor suggests otherwise. "What if they did love you, but the love they authentically offered wasn't wise?"

Reconnecting Love with Wisdom
When we began this book, we noticed the wise teaching that wisdom is a love.

How long, O simple ones, will you *love* being simple? How long will scoffers *delight* in their scoffing and fools *hate* knowledge (Prov. 1:22)?

Since those opening pages, we left off with love (so it seems), and we focused on the relational wisdom arising from the companions and houses we've known.

In this chapter, we must go back now, pick up this thread of love, and weave it into wisdom's fabric. For though wisdom wasn't part of my generation's talk, the idea of love danced upon the lips of nearly every adult and peer, song and movie I knew. Every companion and house I've ever known has wanted to love and be loved.

Wisdom seemed unattractive to us, like an old, frowning, cane-walker.

But love? Ah ... love was untamed. A ravishing stallion, a muse of mystery, the maker of happiness.

But all of us, in our pursuit of love, made a grave error. It never occurred to us that love and wisdom must not be separated. We thought we could prize the one while being deficient in the other.

In contrast, the earliest Christians wove love and wisdom together. They prayed that their "love may abound more and more, *with knowledge and all discernment*" (Phil. 1:9).

We learn from them.

> 1. Through Jesus the love we long for is real and possible (*that your love may abound more and more*).
> 2. Through Jesus the love we long for must tether itself to wisdom (*with knowledge[69] and all discernment[70]*).

Likewise, when blessed by an increase in love among Jesus-followers, Paul instinctively prays that God may give them "the Spirit of wisdom ... having the eyes of their hearts enlightened" (Eph. 1:15-18). An increase in love requires a corresponding increase in what is wise.

Love *is* a wild stallion! But what if the only whisperer the wild stallion of satisfying love willingly trots toward is wisdom?

We all want love, but nearly all of us have been broken by our quest for it. We find ourselves in therapists' and pastors' offices because others didn't love us or because we didn't love them.

What if the horse of love keeps bucking us off and bruising us because wisdom is the only rider true love enjoys? What if the love that gallops like an abounding stallion wild and free, must be sustained by sapient blood, wise muscle, sage bone?[71]

Back in the generation of my wisdom deficit, psychoanalyst and philosopher Eric Fromm described the damaging relational consequences of hallowing love without a wiser apprenticeship to it. Eric was not a follower of Jesus but he echoed this biblical connection between love and wisdom.

"There is hardly any activity, any enterprise, which is started with such tremendous hopes and expectations, and yet, which fails so regularly, as love," Fromm said.[72] We're all "starved for love," yet "hardly anyone thinks that there is anything to be learned about love."[73]

> Almost everything else is considered to be more important than love: success, prestige, money, power—almost all our energy is used for the learning of how to achieve these aims, and almost none to learn the art of loving.[74]

Fromm's plea? We must begin with love as with "any other art, say music, painting, carpentry ... medicine or engineering." Love requires learning, knowledge, skill, time, and practice. Without such wisdom, we who starve for love remain constantly malnourished.

But where does one turn to learn this wisdom of love? Wisdom beckons us.

> Let not steadfast love and faithfulness forsake you; bind them around your neck;
> write them on the tablet of your heart (Prov. 3:3).

The kind of love the wise choose reflects the kind of love God provides and cherishes (steadfast and faithful).[75] Sages want their students to receive this God-love and take this God-love with them wherever they go as if Moses' tablet of God's law of love has reshaped their hearts.[76] His love is what they've received. His love is what they offer us as if God's love is a necklace the wise wear with whomever they meet. The necklace of God's love is His gift of delight for us. And yet His love is also something we wear and is made visible to others.

Exposing our Unwise Relational Instincts

Consider the companions we've explored together. Imagine you say: I feel hurt. I long for a different way of relating. Can we talk?

- A naive heart responds, *"Nothing's wrong. Everything's fine. There's nothing to be hurt about or talk about. I bought you something. Here are some Scriptures."* A naive lover robs us of our tears because naive hearts relish naivete and reach for it when relating to you. It cannot weep when you weep because it loves not to. When your tears are on the menu, naivete doesn't want them.

- A foolish heart responds, *"You're the one who's wrong! You want to talk about pain? I'll tell you about pain."* Folly robs our point of view and experience because it relishes and reaches for foolish ways when relating to you. A foolish heart admonishes, corrects, or instructs those who weep because this is what folly loves to do.

- A scoffer responds, *"Everything is wrong. Everything is pain. Pain is joy. Wrong is pleasure. You're nothing in this world."* Scoffers tear down joy and intensify our weeping because a scoffing heart genuinely finds happiness when robbing your dignity.

- A heart that is broken apart responds, *"You probably hate me. I know it. You hate everything about me. End our relationship I'll understand. I've been through that before. I'll get through it."*

    Hearts broken apart trust their pain, more than they trust the wiser love that can heal them. They protect themselves from those who weep and grow suspicious of those who rejoice because they've grown to relish this kind of protection even though wise healing could be theirs.

    So, if a loved one says, "I feel hurt. I long for a different way of relating. Can we talk?", how would a wiser love respond? Something like:

- *"I hate the thought I've hurt you. It must have taken courage to risk sharing your pain like that. I'm tempted to feel defensive, but I don't want to. I want you and I to be solid together. Would you feel comfortable telling me more about what seems wrong? I want to slow down, hear you, and find our way together."*

Granted, these words may sound formulaic or trite in this moment. But the wise in action are anything but trite, and the point of contrast remains.

Wiser love won't rob you of your tears, your story, your dignity, or your wounds. When in the presence of a wiser heart, you experience what it feels like to be authentically seen and genuinely known as you are without being minimized, slandered, or exaggerated. This is because a wise heart relishes wise things and reaches for them.

To love authentically from the heart only blesses us to the degree that the heart we love you with authentically loves wisdom.

The One Greater than Solomon

If our hearts crave unwise people, places and things, what hope is there?

Jesus.

Take a second look at how Jesus discipled Peter. But now do so by seeing Jesus' way with Peter in light of this menu of loves. See yourself in Peter's shoes and you'll see the ways Jesus trusts to heal you.

Peter's Loves	Jesus' Wisdom Response
Naivete: Lord, I am ready to go with you both to prison and to death (Luke 22:33).	*Wondrous invitation in the brought low places:* "I have prayed for you ... when you have turned again, strengthen your brothers" ... the rooster crows (Luke 22:32-34).

Folly: And Peter took him aside and began to rebuke him, saying, "Far be it from you, Lord! This shall never happen to you" (Matt. 16:22).	*Subversive Bewilderment* "Get behind me, Satan" (Matt. 16:23)!
Scoffing: And one of them struck the servant of the high priest and cut off his right ear (Luke 22:50; John 18:10).	*Confrontation:* No more of this (Luke 22:51)!
Newly Broken: And when the ten heard it, they began to be indignant at James and John (Mark 10:41).	*Near Presence, Gentle Instruction:* And Jesus called them to him and said to them ... (Mark 10:42).
Broken Apart: While Jesus sweat like blood, Peter was sleeping with sorrow (Luke 22:45). He went out and wept bitterly (Luke 22:62).	*Question and Exhortation:* Why are you sleeping? Rise and pray that you may not enter into temptation (Luke 22:46). *Presence, Eye Contact, Quiet:* And the Lord turned and looked at Peter (Luke 22:61).
Broken Open: Peter was grieved because he said to him the third time, "Do you love me?" ... "Lord, you know everything; you know that I love you" (John 21:17).	*Questions, Food, Presence, The Brought Low Place, Revived Love and Purpose:* "Feed my sheep" (John 21:17).

Let's focus now on how Jesus relates to Peter in John 21. After the rooster's crow as Peter staggered bitterly back to his home, Jesus "revealed himself *in this way*" (John 21:1). In Jesus' healing way with Peter, we begin to experience Jesus' healing way with us, when we too authentically loved the things that damaged the very love we longed for.

1. Jesus will remind you of your beginnings with Him.
Huddled near home, Peter threw his grief like a net into the sea, "but that night they caught nothing" (John 21:3).

Wait, hasn't Peter lived this scene already (Luke 5:1-11)? Yes! The one who holds all things together orders a providential repeat, an event in this moment to remind Peter of an earlier one, when Jesus first called Peter.

Is there a place in the world that feels most like home? Do you remember when you and Jesus first met? Why would Jesus bring you this candlelight of memory amid the power outage of your fragmented loves?

Jesus' wisdom. He reveals Himself *in this way.*

2. Jesus will replay scenes of your life with Him.
Next, recognizing Jesus, Peter "threw himself into the sea" (John 21:7). We can barely forget an earlier Peter, the boat, wind and waves and water-walk (Matt. 14:22-36). Do you remember acts of faith when you stepped toward Jesus, and in over your head He reached for you?

Then Jesus breaks bread with fish (John 21:9). How could Peter and the others look at Jesus breaking bread with fish without remembering earlier wonders (John 6:1-14; Luke 24:35)?

What wonders amid the ordinary has Jesus given you that changed the way you saw Him?

And now, this chapter reads like an old episode of *This is Your Life*, in which scenes from our past are paraded in front of us.

The charcoal fire has been crackling this whole time. The Greek word occurs elsewhere only once (John 18:18), when Peter denied Jesus. Someone else lit that original charcoal fire, but this fire Jesus lit. Jesus reveals Himself *in this way.*

What we most want is the denial or removal of this rooster crow and flame from our lives. But craving naive and foolish plates that avoid Jesus within the "brought low" places of life is part of what brought us here in the first place. Jesus wants Peter to see more of Him amid every foul-crow and denial, like one who learns to regard the moon more than the shadows that lurk beneath it. Jesus intends this for us too.

3. Jesus will remind you of your name.

"Simon, son of John" (John 21:15). How long had it been since Peter heard "Simon, son of John" on Jesus' lips? Two years?

If my Mom called me "Zachary Wayne," she had my attention.

Simon Son of John is Peter's birth name. The name before he and Jesus met. The name before Jesus' nickname of affection and calling.

Jesus has Peter's attention.

I'm "Zack, son of Vern and Jan." What's your name, the name you had when you were a child and helpless in the world?

Jesus wants us to hear our names on his lips. We who've made a mess of the menu must learn to think of who we've been and who we are in relation to who Jesus is and always has been for us.

With His name on Peter's lips, Jesus now draws near to the turmoil behind Peter's eyes.

4. Jesus will recover you to wiser love.

Not, "Simon, do you *believe* me?"

Peter's creedal wisdom with worldviews and the search isn't what crushed him.

Not, "Simon will you *use your gifts* for me and prove yourself?"

Peter's wisdom skills and his knack for ministry or fishing were solid.

"Simon Son of John, do you *love* me?"

Peter's faith wreckage stemmed from his captivated heart, the authentic craving that Adam and Eve, the guests of folly's house, the rich young ruler, and so many of us have known. Peter authentically loved what was foolish and this foul love betrayed God, those he loved, and himself.

Jesus is here. Near to you He has a question of love for you.

Do you *love* me?
Do you love *me*?
Do *you* love me?

In this way, dear reader, Jesus reveals Himself and He repairs us by it.

5. *Jesus will empower you to look at old things a new way*
"Feed my sheep," Jesus says.

Fall out of love with the cravings that crushed you. Minister again but with a different heart. Live again as a wiser whisperer calling the stallion of love to your life.

Jesus intends Peter to break open not apart.

What are we saying? After coming to terms with where you're from, reliving how you and Jesus met, the wonder and the needed rescues of His being with you, what your name is, His confronting the pain of your charcoal-fire sins, and confessing the condition of disordered loves within your soul, Jesus revives your purpose, time, choices, and relationships.

"Feed my sheep."

Yet, a fly still buzzes around Peter's head and distracts him.

"But what about John?" Peter asks (John 21:20-23). Peter is like a dog easily unhinged into chase by a squirrel. Within the loving presence of your Master, is there someone you regularly snap your collar to chase?

"If it is my will that he remain ... what is that to you?" Jesus says (John 21:22).

Even forgiven people can repeat what breaks them. Roosters are rarely one-morning creatures. Jesus repeats the grace words with gracious provision and pointed exclamation. "You follow me!"

And by that, Jesus brings Peter's life full circle, a reset, back to first things.

Jesus reveals Himself *in this way.*

Seek the Company of Wisdom

Imagine a day in the company of sages.

"Can you tell us how to reconnect wisdom and love?" we ask.

One of them nods yes.

"This is the compass we offer."

She steps forward, and asks, "What is your purpose in life?"

The rest of the company startles us with loud unison.

> My purpose in life is to love God with all my heart, mind, soul and strength; and out of that prior love, to love my neighbor as myself, no matter who that neighbor is, even if he or she is my enemy (Matt. 5:44; Luke 10:27).

At this, the sages go silent, each of them gazing at us with Christmas morning faces; that wondrous childlike moment just before the presents are opened.

I'm stumped and still weirded out by their creepy all-at-once recitation. But you've caught on quicker than I have. You've got that Christmas morning face too but I'm more lost than ever. You turn to our wise companions.

"You believe the wisdom of Jesus, that we find our greatest purpose when we love God and people, as ourselves, including our enemy?"

Their countenance brightens like a hopeful teacher whose student is about to rightly answer what has before eluded her.

"But," you continue, "*What kind* of love is Jesus talking about? *What kind* of weather in the heart is He assuming?"

Their eyes glisten.

Your confidence grows.

"Am I to say, 'My purpose in life is to *naively* love God with all my heart, mind, soul and strength'; and out of that prior *naive* love, to *naively love* my neighbor as myself, no matter who that neighbor is, even if he or she is my enemy?"

Or "My purpose in life is to *foolishly* love God with all my heart, mind, soul and strength; and out of that prior *foolish* love, to *foolishly love* my neighbor as myself, no matter who that neighbor is, even if he or she is my enemy?"

Or ...

At this, our sage crew interrupts with celebration. Laughter and pats on the back; the glad acknowledgment of a grace-step taken, the contented sense that a light of ancient wisdom has peeked through our window enveloping all of us into its glow.

Part Two

Skillfully Wiser with Jesus

7

Making Better Decisions

Love and do what you will.[77]

Monks deliberated late into the night asking "Which virtue matters most?"

"Fasting and prayer," one said.

"Solitude" another countered.

"Sacrificial acts of service," a third contended.

At last, Anthony answered by telling a story.

> Once, death confronted two friends. To prove great faith, these two friends entered the desert foodless, saying 'God will provide.'
>
> After enduring scorching days without nourishment, these two starving friends were found by desert dwellers who did not believe in Jesus but nonetheless brought them aid. The first friend welcomed their help as God's mercy. But the second friend foolishly refused. He'd wait for God alone, certain that God wouldn't provide needed aid through unbelieving hands. The second friend died.[78]

Discernment, Anthony concluded, is the most vital virtue in a Christian's life (Prov. 16:21; 14:8). Even love must be wise.

What is Discernment?

Discerners are like miners doing the slow-down work[79] of sifting through appearances of creek-bed sediment to separate real from fool's gold (John 7:24).[80] Without discernment we hold onto or let go of the wrong things (1 Thess. 5:21).

"Does this taste like chlorine?" Jessica asked.

"I'm sure it's fine," I say.

"Wait," Jessica says, hurriedly tapping *shrimp tastes like chlorine* into her phone.

A naive lover asks why discernment is necessary. For one thing, failing to discern fresh from sickened shrimp, worsens an evening!

But more so.

As Christians we desire to follow God's leading. Why is decision-making so hard?

1. There are Forgeries in the Fallen World.

A snake slithers in Eden's grasses. Folly mimics Wisdom's house. Phrases like "This isn't right" or "I was wrong" remain necessary under the sun.

2. There's a Fog in our Finite Minds.

There's a lot we don't know about God[81] or ourselves.[82] Listen to the Apostle Paul.

> Constrained by the Holy Spirit not knowing what will happen to me ... *(finite)*

> ... the Holy Spirit testifies to me in every city that imprisonment and afflictions await me *(fallen)* (Acts 20:22-23).

But why do we have to make hard decisions if God is already with us?

3. There's a flow to wisdom's story.[83]

We're neither at creation nor the fall, and we live this side of Jesus' cross and empty tomb. We want to choose perfectly, never having to say, "I was wrong," "I don't know," or "I'm afraid." But we're not in heaven yet.

If the Lord Wills

Because of these fallen and finite challenges, and the fact that God's story is not yet completed, the wise teach two reminders.

First, we can't know what will succeed. "You do not know which will prosper, this or that" (Eccles. 11:6), so try the options given you.

Second, decisions are subject to evil times and sudden ends.

> no one knows his time: like fish caught in a cruel net or like
> birds caught in a trap, so people are trapped in an evil time as
> it suddenly falls on them (Eccles. 9:11-12, CSB)

Missionary friends had to come home before they started. A decade of dreams, "led by the Lord," died on arrival because their host country declared a time of war not peace.

I told you this plan was a waste, folly says. But God didn't wait until they reached the summit of their plan before He'd join them. God lived with them every step of the way. The thwarting of our plans never means the thwarting of God's presence or purpose. Those friends are serving areas they never imagined now, because of the languages they know, and the trust in God they've learned.

Our first point? It's naive or foolish to say, "this is what we planned" and then convince others these plans are God's will. Wiser ones say, "This is our plan as best as we can see. Now let's discover day by day which parts of it are from our Lord and will come to pass" (James 4:13-16).

But now that we know our plans are in God's hands, we need help to make better plans to begin with.

Wisdom's Questions for Decision-Making

As a college student, I led a charity event. Two days before the event, I quit. I'd received a last-minute concert invitation for my original songs. I'd found a substitute leader, but in my haste I didn't account for things going wrong. I returned from ministering to others to damaged friendships and lost trust.

My dorm director graciously commended my songwriting. The problem wasn't the concert itself but the way I went about it and the fact that I hadn't included keeping my word in my definition of choosing "spiritual work" (Prov. 11:3).

"But God blessed it," I said.

"I've no doubt," he said. "But God blessing others when you sing doesn't mean you handled us or our sponsors well."

I didn't know then what you and I have been learning. Being wise in one area of life doesn't make us wise in every area.

There's more, too. In my wisdom deficit, I'd asked only one decision-making question. The wise teach their students to ask at least five.

> Whoever keeps a command will know no evil thing, and the wise heart will know the proper time and the just way. For there is a time and a way for everything ... (Eccles. 8:5-6).

Notice the questions derived from this text.

1. Is this a wise thing? (Whoever keeps a command will know no evil thing.)

Not all who "command" are kind, true or wise. But wisdom's manner is like a wise father or mother, who humbly love God, desire our good, and guide us by their relational love (Prov. 6:20).

When God's commands say "no," we pray for empowerment, not answers.

Must we ask God whether to put folly in charge of others? No.

> Like an archer who wounds everyone
> is one who hires a passing fool or drunkard (Prov. 26:10).

Instead, we ask God's empowerment to trust God's wisdom even though fools pressure us and our naive hearts don't want to appear mean.

But what if God's written word says, "Yes?"

Then, we ask God for prudence, not permission. Permission is already given.

> Go, eat your bread with joy, and drink your wine with a merry heart, *for God has already approved* what you do. Let your garments always be white. Let not oil be lacking on your head. Enjoy life with the wife whom you love ... because that is your portion in life and in your toil at which you toil under the sun. Whatever your hand finds to do, do it with your might ... (Eccles. 9:7-10).

What are these good things which God has "already approved?"

- *food and drink* (eat . . . drink)
- *The joy these provide us* (with joy . . . with a merry heart)
- *bodily necessities* (your garments . . . your head)[84]
- *marriage* (as a married man enjoy life with the wife whom you love)
- *work* (your toil)
- *temperament and interests* (whatever your hand finds to do, do it with your might)

If God's Word has said no or yes and we continue groping about complaining we have no answer from God, wisdom beckons us.

> Have I not written for you thirty sayings
>   of counsel and knowledge,
> to make you know what is right and true ... (Prov. 22:20-21)?

The problem at the charity event wasn't that I chose prohibited things, but that I chose permitted things poorly. I'd asked only one question. Wisdom invites four more.

2. Do I have the wise people I need? Am I one of them? (And the wise heart will know.)
We've looked to God's words for permission.

Now, we look to God's people for perspective.

> The way of a fool is right in his own eyes,
> but a wise man listens to advice (Prov. 12:15; 15:22).

Without wise people, we put ourselves in unsafe situations and fall (Prov. 11:14), which explains why both Moses and Paul look for wise helpers as part of wise planning (1 Cor. 6:5).[85]

Wisdom asks:

1. Are you keeping to yourself, relying solely on your own mind (Prov. 18:1)?

2. Are you avoiding the wiser people who know you best (Prov. 27:6, 9)?

3. Are you avoiding wise advice from expert people in this area of their decision (Prov. 15:2)?

I didn't seek the wiser members of my team or those who knew me best. I turned instead to my newer college peers, who knew little about the situation and less about me. I valued good feedback from concert strangers, but struggled to welcome negative feedback from trusted friends.

3. Is this wise timing? (The proper time ... there is a time for everything.)

Sometimes, like King David or St. Paul, we dream of doing a good and approvable thing, but God says no.

In David's case, "no" meant "no" (2 Sam. 7:1-17).

In Paul's case, "no" meant "wait" (Acts 16:6; 20:18).

A desire biblically commended and wisely counseled, does not mean it is ours to do or that the timing is right.

In my charity event, if I'd suggested a possible change several weeks prior, I likely could have handed off my work with ample time to empower and equip the team. Saying "yes" to the concert could have made sense with that timing. Or I could decline the concert altogether. A fine thing but the wrong time.

4. Is this wisdom's way? (The just way ... there's a way for everything.)

Sages caution their students against "crooked ways" (Prov. 28:6, 18), ways valued by the "man of anger" or "violence" (Prov. 3:31; 22:24-25), that misuse money (Prov. 1:19), sex (Prov. 7:25), or integrity (Prov. 10:9). Wisdom trusts "blameless ways" (Prov. 11:20).

Even sincere people can attempt just things unjustly. We can try to uphold the content of Jesus' words in a manner that opposes the character of Jesus' ways.

Looking back, I lied to my team by using passive language. I said I *could not* lead the charity event rather than I *would not*, as if a circumstance beyond my control forced my exit. I also spiritualized my decision, assigning it greater urgency and importance than was warranted.

Which brings us to wisdom's fifth question.

5. Why do I want this? What is motivating me?
Will I trust this wisdom text from Ecclesiastes 8:6 and its questions or will I dismiss it? Looking back, I didn't want to "miss out." The menu was offered me. I chose a good thing badly while naively demanding that everyone feel happy for me.

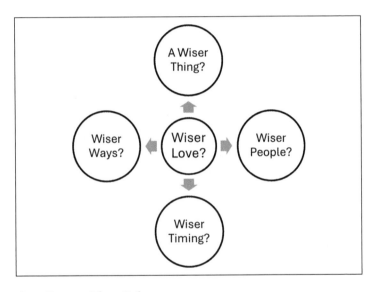

One Greater Than Solomon
In the fullness of His humanity, Jesus faced decisions, too.

Jesus' Dilemma	Jesus' Decision
The tempter came and said to him, "If you are the Son of God, command these stones to become loaves of bread" (Matt. 4:2-3).	It is written. Man shall not live by bread alone but by every word that comes from the mouth of God (Matt. 4:4).

Then the devil took him to the holy city and set him on the pinnacle of the temple and said to him, "If you are the Son of God, throw yourself down, for it is written ... (Matt. 4:5-6).	Again it is written. You shall not put the Lord your God to the test (Matt. 4:7).
Again, the devil took him to a very high mountain and showed him all the kingdoms of the world and their glory. And he said to him, "All these I will give you, if you will fall down and worship me" (Matt. 4:8-9).	It is written, "You shall worship the Lord your God and him only shall you serve" (Matt. 4:10).

Notice *the timing*. Jesus will teach prayer for daily bread and provide bread to the hungry. Eating bread is an approved activity, but this is not the time (4:4).

Notice *the way*. What the devil says is true. The Lord *can* save us. But the devil's proposed plan violates God's way (4:7). A Bible proof-text taken out of context doesn't make it true.

Notice *the thing itself*. We trust what "is written."

Notice *the companions*. Satan is not to be trusted for advice.

Notice *the motivation*. No matter the menu's foolish advantages, God is the one we relish and reach for (4:10).

A Foolish Decision

Years ago, I sat with an American who served as a seminary president outside the U.S.

"How did God call you here?" I asked.

"God didn't," he said. "I made a mistake."

My mouth gaped.

"There's been good fruit despite it all," he continued.

I shifted in my chair.

"You're saying God is faithful and you're fruitful, but mistaken?"

"More than that," he said. "I'd say I was sinful."

I needed a moment to grasp his sentence.

"If God has blessed you, doesn't that mean he led you?"

"God *letting* me serve here doesn't mean he *led* me here," he said. "Don't get me wrong. God still holds me and sovereignly works for my good. But I want to say something if I may."

I nodded yes.

"God being faithful doesn't erase my being foolish. I was ambitious and presumptuous. I didn't count the cost of bringing my family here, the ages and seasons of my kids. I didn't take seriously whether my gifts fit what serves this culture best."

I was puzzled.

He smiled.

"Want some ice cream?"

I did.

I learned that he and the board were planning his exit. Both sides felt their mistake and were trying to care for each other.

Wisdom observes that we typically blame God for self-inflicted choices.

> A person's own foolishness leads him astray,
> yet his heart rages against the LORD (Prov. 19:3 CSB).

But this leader didn't. By grace, he and the board were learning and practicing the humble resilience of wisdom.

> Though a righteous person falls seven times,
> he will get up (Prov. 24:16 CSB).

A Naive Decision

Fast forward three decades.

"I don't understand," the minister said. "God gave us this house."

"How do you know?" I asked.

"Four contracts folded before our bid. It stretched us financially, but we figured interest rates would drop. They didn't. You know that verse about God not giving us scorpions or snakes? I don't buy it anymore."

"What do you mean?" I asked.

"This house is a money pit," he said. "Every week there's something. And our kids … Why is God doing this?"

After a long pause, I gently risked a question.

"Is it possible this isn't God's doing?"

His eyebrows raised.

"What do you mean?"

"Well," I said, "I'm curious why those early contracts folded. If those would-be buyers withdrew their bids because each discovered the house was a money pit, what if those were wisdom clues *not* to buy it?

He cocked his head and sat back.

"Go on," he said.

"I'm hearing you question God's goodness," I said. "But what if you said, 'this house cost too much for us. The interest rates weren't good. The house presented signs of costly work, but we didn't ask about that. We wanted the house and chose it anyway. Now we're encountering the consequences of that choice and having second thoughts.'"

"You're suggesting we did this, not God?"

I shrugged my shoulders.

"Normally, buying a house as a provision from God would have entailed seeking wise counsel, which would have enabled you to better count the cost of necessary hidden repairs, the timing of high interest rates, and the limits of your bank account. Can God provide mysteriously in this scenario? Yes. But if we choose it, as from His hand, it would be because we honestly named the risks, with those who are expert in these matters and with their help we prayerfully counted the cost and made a plan."

He shook his head and chuckled at himself.

Folly and naivete tempt Christians to attribute unwise decisions to God's leading. But doing so robs our ability to say, "I was wrong, naive or a fool." We're like a parent who never does anything wrong because everything we did, even if naive or foolish, was God's leading.

But imagine the healing a child experiences when naive and foolish choosers admit their mistaken choices.[86]

A Broken-Apart Decision

I was asked to consider a job my younger self craved.

Annoyingly, my whole body anxiously jittered as the prestigious inviter spoke.

I tried to avoid the panicky intrusion but I couldn't ignore the anxious floodwaters splashing over the banks of my inner life.

"Well, give it some thought," he said.

But I already knew my answer.

Typically, saying "no" to something we'd like because we're wiser than we once were, doesn't tremble the body. After all, I was in the presence of a friend, not a stranger. I was sitting in an air-conditioned office, not a hospital emergency room or dark alley. I inhabited a time of peace, not war, and nothing outside waited in the day to threaten me.

Yet, in the presence of this good invitation, my body reacted as if I was in danger.

My anxious bodily response arose more likely from an unhealed, broken-apart place—firing signal flares from an inner sinking boat in need of rescue. This job would require me to lead people and institutions still nursing unreconciled misuses of power. My body signaled immediately what my thoughts were taking longer to admit. I was not ready for that.

The wise teach their students to recognize a connection between wisdom and their bodies (Prov. 3:7-8). "A tranquil heart is life to the body" (Prov. 14:30 CSB). "A broken spirit dries up the bones" (Prov. 17:22 CSB).

If I said "yes," I'd do so as one trying not to lose out rather than saying "yes" out of sturdy wholeness, healed freedom, and wise prudence. I needed to say "no," though it meant letting go of a dream my younger self prayed for and foregoing a status my younger self craved.

The Spirit of Wisdom

At this point, someone might ask, "But what about the leading of God's Spirit?"

I've written at length about how to wisely discern promptings, dreams, grieving, quenching, and other matters relating to God's Spirit.[87] For our purpose, consider a wise example and a wise story.

The wisdom example emerges with widows uncared for and ethnicities pained. Notice how early Christians connected the Spirit's leading to the wisdom questions we've just explored (Acts 6:1).

The Twelve summoned the whole company of the disciples and said, "It would not be right for us to give up preaching the Word of God to wait on tables" (Acts 6:2, CSB).[88]	*First, they looked to what God already taught.* Jesus teaches the care of widows, His gospel for the nations, the ministry of Word and service, and how gifted people with shared load support each other.
"Brothers and sisters, select from among you seven men of good reputation, full of the Spirit and wisdom, whom we can appoint to this duty" (Acts 6:3-4, CSB).	*Second, they ask who are the wise people we need?* Wisdom is not limited to leaders. They seek the wise among God's people.

"This proposal pleased the whole company. So they chose ..." (Acts 6:5, CSB).	*Third, they use prudent timing and just ways to make their decision.* No one says, "God told me." Or asks "God, should we care for widows?" or says "God, we won't relieve this poverty and ethnic pain until you give us a sign." Prudence was pleasing.
They had them stand before the apostles, who prayed (Acts 6:6, also v. 4, CSB).	*Fourth, they pray.* Even when permission among approvable things isn't needed, relationship with God is. His presence, provision, power.

How did these early Christians know their plan would work? They didn't. With prudence and prayer amid wise counselors, they decided together, saying "it has seemed good to the Holy Spirit and to us" (Acts 15:28).[89]

Our first point? To follow the questions biblical wisdom provides us *is* to follow the leading of the Spirit of wisdom. To dismiss biblical wisdom in the name of the Spirit of Wisdom who gave it to us, is naive or foolish.

Consider this wisdom story.

Once, Eliphaz, Job's foolish friend, heard an otherworldly spirit whisper messages in a dream.

1. *Was this spirit from God?* Eliphaz didn't bother to find out.

2. *Were Eliphaz's counselors wise? Was Eliphaz wise?* Blind to his own folly, Eliphaz interprets "the spirit" foolishly, to justify the log in his eye. An interpretation his foolish counselors commended.

3. *Was this the right way?* Eliphaz has long let go of sackcloth, ashes, and the tears of friendship. He tries to correct, admonish and instruct one who bitterly weeps.
4. *Is this the right timing?* Job is physically and mentally overcome by suffering.
5. *Why did Eliphaz do this?* He loved folly more than wisdom.

The supernatural dream was real, but naively regarded and foolishly discerned. In God's name, Eliphaz harmed Job (Job 4:12-16). God rebuked Eliphaz for it (Job 42:7).

Wisdom's students begin with caution, therefore, not with God who acts supernaturally, but with those who make much of their own multiplied dreams and experiences in God's name while bypassing wisdom's menu of loves and discernment process.[90]

But the wise would correct any notion of seeking the Spirit's leading without trusting the Spirit's written wisdom. We only know the five wisdom questions we're asking because they were given to us by the Spirit in the words the Spirit inspired.

Do you remember our "menu-of-loves" text? Notice God's promise that follows.

> How long, O simple ones, will you love being simple?
> How long will scoffers delight in their scoffing
>   and fools hate knowledge?
>   If you turn at my reproof,
> behold, I will pour out my spirit to you;
>   I will make my words known to you (Prov. 1:22-23).

Wisdom teaches us to admit fault and turn to His wiser love. This menu-of-loves correction is part of how God leads us.

1. God showers us with His intimacy and presence (I will pour out my Spirit to you).

2. God illumines His love-written words for us (I will make my words known to you).

The Grace of His Wisdom

Jesus describes a young man who left home unwisely.

> 'Father, *give me the share of property that is coming to me*' (Luke 15:12).

It is wise for a child to grow and eventually leave home to begin his own life. But the young man's way of doing a fine thing, communicated disrespect and created unnecessary pain. His timing didn't help either.

> *Not many days later*, the younger son gathered all he had and took a journey into *a far country* ... (Luke 15:13).

The young man was impatient toward a later season's good provision (his share of inheritance). He also distanced himself from the wisdom community that rooted him. The naive community he chose instead applauded his wisdom deficits but abandoned him in his difficulties (Luke 15:15).

Coming to his senses, he'd have to admit he'd relished and reached for unwise loves and had let go of the wise love so freely given him.

> he squandered his property in reckless living ... he had spent everything ... (Luke 15:13-14).

The young man experienced first-hand how a wise thing, implemented with unwise ways, timing, people, and motivations, wrecks the very happiness and love we're trying to find.

But the story doesn't have to end here. Jesus tells us more.

The Father's *way* is longsuffering. His is a running-toward-us kind of love, full of a no-regret-forgiveness, abounding in welcome.

The Father's *people* though having experienced our worst, will, because of His grace toward them, still welcome us home with hearty celebration.

The Father's *timing* is immediate with lavish love but patient to wait for the young man, just as He waits for us.

Perhaps a realization gently takes hold of your hand.

"We've been studying discernment all along, haven't we, since the first pages of this book?"

Whether entering the wisdom deficit of our life stories in chapter one, or sitting by the well with the naive woman in chapter two. When with the foolish lawyer, the scoffing religious leaders, or Peter's bitter weeping in chapters three through five or our menu of loves in chapters six.

Jesus has been discerning the differences between our naive, foolish, and scoffing companions, houses, and hearts, whether broken apart or broken open.

He's been teaching us to detect "the inner meaning of appearances" and come again "to know the inner workings of God's love and our unique place in the world."[91]

Why would the One Greater than Solomon do this for us?

Because His wisdom is a love.

And His wise love is not against us, but for us.

8

Anchoring Your Life in God's Steadfast Love

*The world was once alive and enchanted,
quivering with the love of God.*[92]

A young man palms his stressing eyes.

"Is she the one?" he asks.

The young man is pondering a core question of life.

He seeks your advice.

"What if God is looking at me angry because I'm not choosing what He wants? I'm trying to read His signs. But what if I mess this decision up?"

You nod your head. You feel his angst. You ask if he's heard of wisdom's five decision-making questions. Prayerfully, you begin to ask them together over a month of visits.

You begin with question number one. "Is it the right thing to marry or remain single?"

You both study what the Spirit of Wisdom has written. You discover that either path, if chosen *in the Lord* is approved already. The man and his girlfriend can *do as they want*, wisely assessing their circumstances and prudently choosing according to what each has *decided in his heart* (1 Cor. 7:36-37, 39).

But the following week, something troubles you as you walk through wisdom's second question with the man. You notice it as the two of you are exploring questions like:

- When you're with her are you wise with love or prone to a more naive, foolish, or broken-apart version of yourself?

- In what areas of life is your girlfriend wise? In what areas of life is she naive, foolish, tempted to scoff, or broken apart?

- Who are the people in your life wise with marriage and singleness? Would you be willing to listen? Would she?

The young man feels pressure, not delight or joy. It's as if God sent the young man to his room to figure this decision out by himself while God marches back out into the hall toward the living room, shouting,

"Don't come out here till you've decided."

God then adds guilt-laden syllables of expectation.

"I'm sure you'll choose what I've always taught you is best for you."

Suddenly, it dawns on you. The thing missing in this decision is love.

The young man is trying to decide a core importance in his life while having no felt sense of God's love for him. He's by himself alone until he makes his decision. Only after he walks out the lonely hallway into the living room of expectations will he know whether God will have affection for him or not.

But his wiser mentors will remind him.

What is desired in a man is steadfast love (Prov. 19:22).

When we begin our apprenticeship with the wise, they establish "steadfast love" as our life purpose. Steadfast love is the kind of love that God possesses and gives. What we've called "wise love" on the menu.

Sitting there with the young man you realize that wisdom's five questions are meant to be tethered to wisdom's purpose for our lives. Tethered that is, to the steadfast love of God.

One Greater than Solomon

In our last chapter, we observed how Jesus addressed wisdom's five questions when discerning and deciding in the wilderness.

Pause here. Go back now. Take a second look. Notice how the steadfast love of God envelops the entire scene.

Jesus as a Discerner	Decisions in the Wilderness
Jesus is loved by the Father.	And behold, a voice from heaven said, "This is my beloved Son, with whom I am well pleased" (Matt. 3:17).
Jesus is led by the Spirit of God.	Jesus was led up by the Spirit (Matt. 4:1).
Jesus is not yet in the final chapter of the story.	Into the wilderness to be tempted by the devil ... (Matt. 4:1).
It is written.	Man shall not live by bread alone but by every word that comes from the mouth of God (Matt. 4:4).
Again, it is written.	You shall not put the Lord your God to the test (Matt. 4:7).
It is written.	You shall worship the Lord your God and him only shall you serve (Matt. 4:10).
Jesus is not alone but ministered to. This scene isn't the only or last scene of His part in the story.	Behold angels came and were ministering to him (Matt. 4:11).

Jesus reveals in His practice the moment-by-moment attention to divine love that the wise teach their students.

> Whoever is wise, let him attend to these things;
> let them consider the steadfast love of the Lord (Ps. 107:43).

The devil is there, as well as hunger, thirst, and isolation.

But the wise of heart discern that God's steadfast love is there too, invisible as it may seem. The wise take hold of it and are carried by it.

Whether you're asking, "Is she the one," or "Do I take this job?" or "What do I do with my estranged child?" Take a deep breath.

Amid all you don't know, consider what you do know. God loves you. Let the grace words spoken over Jesus by the Father, be spoken over you, through Jesus (John 15:9-11; 16:26-27).

You can say something like:

> I don't yet know the answer to my dilemma.
> But I do know this.

> In Christ,
> I'm loved by the Father
> I'm led by His Spirit
> I'm not in heaven yet, but
> I'm not alone. I'm ministered to and this moment isn't the only or last scene in my story.

Deciding As One Already Loved

Imagine a child in her grandmother's home.

"May I read this book?" the child says.

"Yes, dear," the grandmother responds. "You may freely read or play with any book, toy, or game in this room."

A few minutes later, the grandchild asks again.

"May I play with this train?"

Anchoring Your Life in God's Steadfast Love

"Yes, dear, I'm here with you. You may freely read or play with anything you find here."

Minutes later, the grandchild asks again about a different toy, and then again.

The child does nothing wrong by enjoying this room of provisions within the present and permissive delight of her grandmother. The grandmother isn't tricking the child by inflicting a desperate task of choosing *the one right toy or else*. The grandmother finds joy in the child's presence and play, in their relationship, and their time together.

So, if the child chooses the blue train, the grandmother gladdens. "Your older brother loved that one too. He liked the shiny bell. What do you like about it?"

If the child chooses the raggedy *Mike Mulligan and His Steam Shovel* book, the grandmother laughs and says, "Your old grandpa loved this book so much as a boy, that he has always had a copy ready for his children and grandchildren to read. Shall we read it together?"

If the child chooses this car with that blanket and that dinosaur and then makes up a story using the car, the blanket and the dinosaur as characters, the grandmother giggles with joy. "Oh, my," she says. "What a wonder you are. I love the stories you create."

Perhaps the child ventures a question of relational delight, too.

"What do you like in this room, Mi-maw?"

"Well, now. Let me see. Do you see that teddy bear? Once in days that will seem old and ancient to you, I ..."

Isn't this like God gifting Adam and Eve every tree but one?

If they'd said, "God, should I pick fruit from that approved tree first and then pick from this one? Then, should we make pie, or just cut the fruit into slices?"

Like the grandmother with her grandchild, God would say, "Dear ones, you needn't ask. I'm with you. We're together. I've already approved."

We try to introduce this steadfast love to the young man anguished and asking, "Is she the one?"

"Whatever you and she decide," we say to him, "One thing you know for sure. You're both loved with a steadfast never-quitting love. You belong to a people. God has given you already approvable things. His love is your life purpose. What is desired, whether single or married, is that you are founded and formed in His steadfast love."

"I feel a weight sort of lifting," he might say. "But I'm scared. I don't know what to do with that kind of freeing love you're talking about."

"I feel that too," we might say. "But we're trying to anchor your decision, not with God as your harsh taskmaster from whom you must slavishly fear and hide.[93] Rather, God is a good father and you are His child already and dearly loved" (Eph. 5:1). We want to learn how "a wise lover regards not so much the gift of him who loves, as the love of him who gives."[94]

Many of us face decisions as if all we have is ourselves, famished and alone, encircled by wild beasts and devils in the wilderness. But the Spirit of Wisdom's five questions provide clues, not condemnation. *We aren't making decisions to get God's love. We're making decisions because we already have God's love.*[95]

Learning to Attend and Consider

So, if we hope to discern God's steadfast love on the menu and make decisions as those anchored by this love because God's steadfast love expresses the desired purpose of our life, where do we start?

We begin by returning to this wisdom text.

> Whoever is wise, let him attend to these things;
> let them consider the steadfast love of the LORD (Ps. 107:43).

The wise will apprentice us to "attend to" and "consider" any glimpse of God's steadfast love we can find each day. We get a sense of what an attentive-to-love kind of life looks like by analogy with an artist who draws.

> The Sketch Hunter ... moves through life as he finds it, not passing negligently the things he loves, but stopping to know them, and to note them down in the shorthand of his sketchbook ... or on his drawing pad. Like any hunter he hits or misses. He is looking for what he loves, he tries to capture it. It's found anywhere, everywhere. Those who are not hunters do not see these things. The hunter is learning to see and to understand—to enjoy.[96]

This description of "looking for what He loves" in order to capture it, understand it and enjoy it, is a helpful way of describing what it means to wisely attend and consider the steadfast love of the Lord.

The Psalmists, for example, turn nearly every situation they face into a meditation on God's love for them. There are so many verses on God's steadfast love that for our purpose I'm limiting what I quote to the Psalms, and this without referencing three entire psalms devoted entirely to God's steadfast love for us (107, 118, 136).

To learn a wiser life, we begin attending to His steadfast love when we awake each morning.

Attend to His Steadfast Love in the Morning[97]

> Satisfy us in the morning with your steadfast love,
> *that we* may rejoice and be glad all our days (Ps. 90:14).

The words, "that we," tell you that you can make it all your days, go the distance in your life with gladness, when you know you're loved. Knowing God's steadfast love is the source that empowers you to rejoice and be glad day upon day throughout all your days.

So, you wake up in the morning fragmented, distracted, criticized, discontented, hurried into activity. The first thing is to plead the scarcity within your soul. Don't stop at "Help me *believe* your steadfast love." Move farther into the experience of it. Ask to be *satisfied* by His steadfast love.

Ask also to *hear* of His steadfast love (Ps. 143:8) and then, dear friend, learn to *sing* of it (Ps. 59:16).

By the time you reach for your phone, check your task list, respond to email, begin to study, or keep your first appointment, His steadfast love is already becoming your meditation. It anchors your day, reshapes your vision, empowers you to walk faithfully into what awaits you.

> For your steadfast love *is before my eyes,*
> and I walk in your faithfulness (Ps. 26:3).

But how? What if we don't feel His steadfast love in the morning?

I know miserable experiences like this, too. Sometimes I greet the morning like a troubled atheist, lost in a God-empty story that cannot handle what frightens me. In the words of Phillip Larkin's haunting poem, "Aubade," I wake up staring into "soundless dark … unresting death," experiencing "a special way of being afraid" amid "all the uncaring intricate rented world."[98]

On such mornings, I need the name of Jesus spoken and His true story told me afresh. I grab a pencil from the lampstand and scribble grace-words on a page.

*'The spell of night-tales broken,
at the name of Jesus spoken,
and I am myself again."*

It is only 5:56 am. But I've already fought a battle for first love. By remembering who God is toward us.

> The LORD is gracious and merciful,
> slow to anger and abounding in steadfast love.
> The LORD is good to all,
> and his mercy is over all that he has made (Ps. 145:8-9; 86:15; 103:8, 11, 17).

Cherishing God's Love Tokens

This means we do not fight this morning's battle for wise love alone. The God of steadfast love precedes us. He was awake while we slept. His eternal love happily works the night shift. He furnishes His creation and His providence with what Charles Spurgeon called, God's "love tokens."[99] Spurgeon says:

> Suppose that as you wake up one morning, you find lying upon your pillow a precious love-token from your unknown friend, a ring sparkling with jewels and engraved with a tender inscription, a bouquet of flowers bound about with a love-motto! Your curiosity knows no bounds. But you are informed that this wonderous being has not only done for you what you have seen, but a thousand deeds of love which you did not see, which were higher and greater still as proofs of his affection.
>
> Not only this, but imagine you are further told that in his love for you, your friend fought battles to keep them from you and to keep you safe.
>
> He was wounded, and imprisoned, and scourged for your sake, for he had a love to you so great, that death itself could not overcome it; you are informed that he is every moment occupied in your interests, because he has sworn

by himself that where he is there you shall be; his honors you shall share, and of his happiness you shall be the crown.

In light of such good news, that we are the object of an "ancient love," a "mighty love," a "wise all-seeing love," only a naive or foolish, a scoffing or broken apart heart could say, "how nice," and then go on.

Wiser loves beckon us to feel our thirst deepen by thoughts of it. We respond to His tokens of love with love of our own.

If you see him, tell him I am sick [with] love. The love tokens which he gives me, they stay for a while with the assurance of his affection but they impel me onward with the more unconquerable desire that I may know him. I must know him; I cannot live without knowing him. His goodness makes me thirst and pant and faint and even die that I might know him.[100]

As our hearts grow wiser by this grace of love, and we begin to crave wiser loves on the menu of our lives, how do we do our day differently, once we've begun our morning, hearing and singing of our Lord's steadfast love?

Relocate the True Story Each Morning
1. Remember, you are in God's world.

the earth is full of the steadfast love of the LORD (Ps. 33:5).

2. In this light, put all evil news and taunting back into their proper places.

Why do you boast of evil, O mighty man?
The steadfast love of God *endures all the day* (Ps. 52:1).

Amid lament, righteous anger, or frightened thoughts, relocate the good news.

The steadfast love of the Lord?

> It fills the earth.
> All day long it doesn't quit.
> Ever.
> Who then can boast?

How foolish of evil to think that it stands victorious in this world.

3. Which means that you remember who you are in the morning.

> His delight is not in the strength of the horse,
>   nor his pleasure in the legs of a man,
> but the LORD takes pleasure in those who fear him,
>   in *those who hope* in his steadfast love (Ps. 147:10-11).

Wisdom teaches its students to grow attentive and intentional regarding the love tokens of God for our day.

> At best, the morning rituals of a household support the reality that God loves us and that his love is the defining fact of the universe. Here our habits of waking serve as gospel liturgies that push us into the arms of a father who loves us, and then send us out into the world to love others. But at worst, our habits of waking indulge alternative realities where the universe depends on us and what we do today. This is the gospel of humankind, where our rituals tell us that we have to keep up to survive and turn the household into a school of rush, fear, and frustration. So we must wake up to how we wake up.[101]

God's steadfast love for you, not your effort, forges your hope. His delight and joy in you isn't sparse, or leftover, but "great!" (Ps. 117:2).

4. So, it's time you begin to use the word "my."

> he is *my* steadfast love and *my* fortress,

> *my* stronghold and *my* deliverer,
> *my* shield and he in whom *I* take refuge ... (Ps. 144:2).

Listen to how one old-timer describes what it means to remember that *our* God is *my* God. *Our* Savior is *my* Savior.

> Note especially the pronoun "our" and its significance. You will readily grant that Christ gave Himself for the sins of Peter, Paul, and others who were worthy of such grace. But feeling low, you find it hard to believe that Christ gave Himself for *your* sins ... Make ample use of this pronoun "our." Be assured that Christ has canceled the sins, not of certain persons only, but *your* sins. Do not permit yourself to be robbed of this lovely conception of Christ.[102]

Our point?

It is true that God's steadfast love isn't solely about you, but it does envelop you.

God loves all His people, yes, and you are one of them.

But What If?

Your work seems small or uncertain? Appeal to His steadfast love for you.

> The LORD will fulfill his purpose for me;
> your steadfast love, O LORD, endures forever (Ps. 138:8).

You feel like you're failing? Appeal to His steadfast love.

> When I thought, "My foot slips,"
> your steadfast love, O LORD, held me up (Ps. 94:18).

You feel lost, mocked, undefended? Plead His love.

> Lord, where is your steadfast love of old ... (Ps. 89:49)?

> Has [your] steadfast love forever ceased?
> Are [your] promises at an end for all time (Ps. 77:8)?

There's so much you don't know? Look to His love.

> Deal with your servant according to your steadfast love,
> and teach me your statutes (Ps. 119:124).

You can't seem to find any comfort? His love anchors your hope.

> Let your steadfast love comfort me
> according to your promise to your servant (Ps. 119:76).

You feel worn out, apathetic, spent? Plead His love.

> Give me life according to your steadfast love (Ps. 119:159; 88).

All you want to do is glorify Him? Then dear fellow seeker of wisdom, God's love is your hope!

> Not to us, O LORD, not to us, but to your name give glory, for the sake of your steadfast love and your faithfulness (Ps. 115:1)!

You're lost without rescue? Pray because of His great love!

> Turn, O LORD, deliver my life;
> save me for the sake of your steadfast love. (Ps. 6:4; 109:21, 26; 103:4).

You feel you're not worthy to worship Him? You're right, but for His love!

> But I, through the abundance of your steadfast love,
> will enter your house (Ps. 5:7).

All you can see is your sin? Appeal to His love.

> Remember not the sins of my youth or my transgressions; according to your steadfast love remember me … (Ps. 25:7; Prov. 16:6).

All you can feel are throbbing wounds from being sinned against? Look to His love.

> I will rejoice and be glad in your steadfast love, because you have seen my affliction; you have known the distress of my soul (Ps. 31:7).

You have nothing to offer Him? His love remains yours.

> Give thanks to the God of heaven, for his steadfast love endures forever (Ps. 136:26).

Jesus invites us to notice a bird or a flower, to see in their care the One who cares for us (Matt. 6:28-30). When you pray, Jesus continues, speak intimately to God as a good father who won't give you a scorpion or a snake when what you most need is bread (Luke 11:11-13).

Behold the Grace of His Love

Such steadfast love changed a man like Saul of Tarsus, who took up the Psalmist's baton in Christ. For the Apostle Paul, God's steadfast love in Jesus:

1. Prioritizes what we set our minds on to help us persevere.

> Love bears all things, believes all things, hopes all things, endures all things. Love never ends (1 Cor. 13:1-8).

2. His divine love frames our prayers for each other.

> That you … may have strength to comprehend with all the saints what is the breadth and length and height and depth,

and *to know the love of Christ* that surpasses knowledge, that you may be filled with all the fullness of God (Eph. 3:18-19).

3. His divine love anchors our identity.

I have been crucified with Christ, and I no longer live, but Christ lives in me. The life I live in the body, I live by faith in the Son of God, *who loved me and gave himself for me* (Gal. 2:20 CSB).

(4) His divine love prompts our repentance.

Or do you presume on the riches of his kindness and forbearance and patience, not knowing that God's kindness is meant to lead you to repentance (Rom. 2:4)?

(5) His divine love empowers our obedience.

Imitate God, *as dearly loved children* (Eph. 5:1 CSB).

(6) His divine love enables us to make it no matter what.

Who shall separate us from the love of Christ (Rom. 8:35-39)?

Decisions beckon us daily.

But the steadfast love of the Lord has preceded them, undergirded them, outflanked them, and held us within them.

How lovely God is to the wise! Because the wise of heart perceives God's steadfast love everywhere.

Isn't this why Jesus is precious to us?

"See how He loved," we say.

Isn't this why we so regard the death of Jesus?

"Forgive them," He says.

Isn't His love why the resurrection of Jesus emboldens us?

"Death, sin, and miseries will die, but His love remains."

Isn't this why His coming again aches our hearts with longing? For He is our first and true love.

No wonder it was said by those who knew Him.

"His love for us never quit" (John 13:1).

9

Getting a Better Handle on Time

Time has become disenchanted, stripped of its sacred magic. No one needs God anymore to know what time it is.[103]

A working sculpture keeps time on a Cambridge street corner. Its name is "the Chronophage," which means "Time-eater." Its sharp, shredding edges cut a picture of a grasshopper, transformed from its gentle hop among soft grasses into a famished, dragon-like skeleton. Having pounced upon a clock for its victim, this unsatiated creature relentlessly devours each second of our lives. It was created by John C. Taylor, who said, "Time is a destroyer. Once a minute is gone you can't get it back."[104]

Beneath this vulture of time, a carved Bible verse warns us. "And the world is passing away along with its desires."

The day I watched this beast ravage life, a little girl dared to hunch her shoulders beneath its fanged metal. She made a crook of her little arms by bending her elbows out in front of her. She twisted her wrists and fingers arthritically. She squinched her little face into a ferocious contortion and with her little voice she tried to roar fiercely.

And then? She laughed and giggled, giggled and laughed. She hunched again and roared again, laughed again and giggled again. She had her grandma and all of us giggling, laughing, and playing, too.

The irony made itself plain to any who could behold it. Time is a destroyer. And yet even a child can play with it. As the beast insisted all was lost and too late, the child giggled humanly within the safety of her grandmother's love and the joy all of us felt.

Watching the child playing, an inkling within us says, "Hold on. Something is off."

We search the Bible verse on our phones. And now, we nearly laugh out loud.

"Folly's house is at it again," we say half to ourselves.

"Look, at the whole verse," we say to someone standing beside us.

And the world is passing away along with its desires
But whoever does the will of God abides forever (1 John 2:17).

The time-eater and his earthly creator have censored John the Apostle, mid-sentence. Yes, time is a breath. But folly mimics and lies. For the will of God and those who love God will devour the time-eater, not the other way round. Let the redeemed of the Lord say so.

The Anatomy of a Time-Eaten Life
When I was younger, energy drinks didn't exist. Young people ran circles around the aging. Now, energy drinks are countless and targeted not to middle-age, but to youth.

When did it happen that being young can't provide a person enough energy to get through a day?

In the time-eaten story, God and His steadfast love don't exist. Untethered from an alive God who is with us and loves us, we suffer "time sickness."[105] We begin to imitate the time-eater, take on his mannerisms, feel his sense of scarcity, choose his impatience to consume.

Consider the talk a time-eaten life cultivates.

- Frustrated fatigue: "There aren't enough hours in the day."
- Relentless urgency: "I've got to make the most of my time. Give me another energy drink."
- Painful regret: "I wasted all that time."
- Restless worry: "When will my time come?"
- Anxious fear: "I don't want this time to happen."
- Disillusioned loss: "I thought by now I would have …"
- Loveless loneliness: "No one has time for me."
- Apathetic resignation: "No amount of time will make a difference."
- Dreamless shame: "I missed my chance. That time has sailed."[106]

And sentiments like these on the lips, not just of the middle-aged, but twenty-somethings.

Sage teachers foreshadow the time-eater by warning their students from *striving after wind* (Eccles. 1:14, 17; 2:11, 17, 26; 4:4, 6, 16; 5:16; 6:9).

Wind-striving is a way of being in the world that constantly expends strenuous energy to grasp what cannot be held and will always elude. We speed up life driven by a misguided craving on the menu of loves, "envy" (Eccles. 4:4). To envy is to meditate on not missing out, to want what others have, to expend energy to attain it and outshine them if we can.

Sages warn their students for at least two reasons.

First, we may get the life we wanted but at a cost we did not expect. Sages tell a story about a man who loved money. This man starts a company, works long hours, and attains the wealth and status he strove for, yet he remains unhappy, feeling relationally fractured, lonely, anxious, sick, and angry (Eccles. 5:10-17).

Which leads to the second sage caution. *To fill our hands with anxious striving, we have to let go of a quiet soul.*

> Better is a handful of quietness than two hands full of toil and a striving after wind (Eccles. 4:6).

The wind-striver says, "Look at my two hands full of production and envied achievement."

The wise say, "But you've let go of a quiet soul to attain it. Better to have one hand of earnest labor with one hand of a tranquil mind."

As I write, Starbucks, the coffee chain, faces a challenge.[107] Its vision was to provide a "third space" with lamps, couches, tables and good coffee so that friends and family within an individualized and fractured culture, could linger and experience a sense of friendship and home.

But demand for transactional phone orders and speedy drive-thru service is causing Starbucks to let go of lamps and couches to make ends meet.

Some customers feel happy for efficient on-the-go service. But others complain the loss of relational space. The company's dilemma reveals the larger one within our culture and the point the wise tried to make with their students centuries ago.

To have meaningful relationships and a nourished inner life we have to slow down, take time, linger together in unhurried ways. But slowing down would mean letting go of hastily consuming our seconds so as to produce more tasks in less time, like the time-eater.

Two paths emerge before us.

Jesus tells a story of a man consuming and storing up possessions for himself and telling his soul all is well. The man prepares to retire in happiness.

> But God said to him, "Fool! This night your soul is required of you, and the things you have prepared, whose will they be?" So is the one who lays up treasure for himself and is not rich toward God (Luke 12:19-21).

What Jesus calls "rich toward God," the sages called "quiet of soul." We only have two hands. The only way to hold two hands of toil is by letting go of the work-and-rest rhythm God gave us and instead prizing a work-and-work pace of life.

Rest and Work

A wiser work and rest rhythm differs from a sluggard who conflates laying on the couch with a quiet soul. Both hands are empty—no good work, and no inner nourishment with God.

A wiser work-and-rest rhythm seeks one hand of quiet and one hand of good work, which bothers the time eaten. Won't we miss out?

"Miss out on what?" the wise ask. "Restlessness of soul? A life more lonely, anxious, sick, angry, and sleepless?" Good work tethered by inner rest with God isn't missing out.

> If the iron is blunt, and one does not sharpen the edge,
> he must use more strength, but wisdom helps one to succeed (Eccles. 10:10).

The proverb pictures two farmers trying to succeed.

One pauses. The other doesn't.

The one who pauses works smarter, like cutting an orange with a sharpened knife in contrast to a dull knife which causes one to expend more strength than necessary.

Take note. The wise teach their students that God never meant us to expend more energy than the job requires.

The smarter farmer who kept going by pausing, replenished his animals, land, workers and tools. For a while, he seems to fall behind the farmer who never pauses.

But over time, the never-pausing team, lose their edge and can't keep up. They burn out.

Take note. Thriving work depends upon strategic rest.

Wisdom is no Waste of Time

The only way to speed up and consume more is to let go of the God-given timepieces that would slow us down and fill us up.[108]

Timepieces like rest. But also, the timepieces of ordinary love tokens from God.

> There is nothing better for a person than to eat, drink, and enjoy his work. I have seen that even this is from God's hand, because who can eat and who can enjoy life apart from him (Eccles. 2:24-25 CSB)?

If wisdom students took a quiz, one of the questions would be, "In God's world, what are the best things in life? The few things that when compared to all else would cause us to say, 'There is nothing better' than this" (Eccles. 3:12, 22; 8:15, 9:7-10)?

The wise would say:

Our food and drink that God gives us
Our enjoyment with the work God gives us

And now we're hearkening back to the "already approved" things we discussed in chapter seven.

Our bodily necessities God provides

The wife and husband of our youth if we're married which God gladly approves
Our temperament and interests which God gives us

These are God's ordinary love tokens to us. But the time-eater protests wisdom's "nothing better" idea. The time-eater's only concern is the ticking clock, and therefore it decries ordinary people, everyday food, and learning to derive inner joy with work. These can waste time, feel boring, ordinary or irrelevant. They slow us down.

Wisdom says otherwise. Who can eat or work, or enjoy life apart from God and His steadfast love?

> Everyone to whom God has given wealth and possessions and power to enjoy them, and to accept his lot and rejoice in his toil—this is the gift of God (Eccles. 5:19).

When we remember we're in God's world, that God is alive, and that we are tethered to His steadfast love, a person:

> will not much remember the days of his life because God keeps him occupied with joy in his heart (Eccles. 5:20).

Consequently, the wise deem it no waste of time to pay attention to people, mull over what happens in their lives, and with God in prayer, artistically tell what they saw as a wisdom story to benefit others. "I saw an example of wisdom under the sun," they'll say. Then, they'll tell you a story (Eccles. 9:13-16).

Likewise, sages will call their students to pay attention to insects (Prov. 6:6-11), or a field (Prov. 24:30-34), or animals (Prov. 30:19). They'll tell you how they watched a long while, reflected, and learned from what they saw in God's world.

Everything around you is pressuring you to do large, famous things, as fast as you can.

But almost anything that matters in life will invite you to small, mostly overlooked graces, over a long period of time.[109]

Tending to God's love tokens with the people He's given us to love, the work He's given us to enjoy, and the place He's given us to inhabit is no waste of time; it's the purpose of time.

A God-inhabited story of time means that every second has a sanctuary with God waiting for you within it. Minutes mention Him. Hours hallow Him. Days declare Him. Trees clap for Him. Birds sing of Him. Ants teach of Him.

Each portion of the day and night is God hearing me.

"Morning, noon, and night" I cry out to God (Ps. 55:17-19).

Each portion of the day and night is God adored by me.

Seven times a day I praise you (Ps. 119:164).

Every moment my Maker holds me.
In times of trouble (Ps. 9:9).
In evil times (Ps. 37:19).
My times, all of them, are held within God's hands (Ps. 31:15).

No wonder King David said: The Lord is my Shepherd ... *He makes me lie down* ... (Ps. 23:2). I am like a sheep, David the hardworking King, says. I too fear predators, am anxious about relationships, and feel an awkward inability to lie down and be safe. But God has the wise skill of non-anxious love to rest me. My cup overflows. Which is to say, my inner life is quieted by His presence and love.

One Greater Than Solomon Is Here

Followers of Jesus witnessed His God-inhabited view of time. Jesus could pray spontaneously or sing a hymn as if God was there all along. He'd withdraw for prayer as if God is as near in the night or the morning as He is during the day.

Jesus could rest at noon or in the late afternoon. He'd pause to keep going, as if God's love and our human lives weren't separated, but integral.

Jesus' brothers struggled with Jesus' time-keeping. They urged Jesus to leverage His platform.

> No one works in secret if he seeks to be known openly. If you do these things show yourself to the world (John 7:4).

Jesus responded by contrasting their view of time with His.

> "*Your time* is always here," Jesus says (John 7:6).

Jesus points them to the menu of loves. "The world cannot *hate* you," Jesus says. Which is to say, the world craves what you plan, but "*My time* has not yet come" (John 7:6, 8); what I love differs from what you love. How I inhabit time differs from you.

Consider another occasion. Jesus says:

> When you see a cloud rising in the west, you say at once, 'A shower is coming.' And so it happens. And when you see the south wind blowing, you say, 'There will be scorching heat,' and it happens (Luke 12:54-55).

Jesus commends their wisdom regarding daily time with its seasons and situations. They wisely take an umbrella when it looks like rain or defer work from the afternoon heat by prizing shade. But they've untethered this creational keeping of the clock from the One who gave it to them.

"Hypocrites!" Jesus says. (A startling phrase to expose their time sickness).

You know how to interpret the appearance of the earth and sky, but why do you not know how to interpret the present time? (Luke 12:56).

The kingdom of God is breaking in all around them, but they have no eyes to see it. The sky and its colors offer nothing but leverage to better plan their schedules and minimize hindrances to their goals.

It's as if Jesus says, "You know how to recognize daily and seasonal time. That's good! But why do you not know how to discern God's presence right here before you?"

Jesus invites His students to re-tether time to the living God who gave it to us.

> Time has to be converted ... not just something to get through or manipulate or manage, but the arena of God's work with us. Whatever happens—good things or bad, pleasant or problematic—we look and ask, "What might God be doing here?" ... Time points to Another and begins to speak to us of God.[110]

Wisdom & Time
Wisdom converts our view of time by recovering its fullness.

- *Daily time:* There are four portions of each day: morning, noon, evening, and the night watches. Each portion has its own work with its own cares, carnalities, and consolations, and implements what Jesus meant by taking each day as it comes (Matt. 6:34).[3]

- *Seasonal time:* Biblically, there are two basic seasons in the physical world, wet seasons and dry seasons. These seasons serve as metaphors for life's delightful and disquieting circumstances (Eccles. 3:1-8).

- *Redemptive time:* Months were marked by feasts of past memory and future hope in the Lord, such as the

Passover. Remembering God's actions in the past, and remembering His promises for the future, enable us to interpret and anchor our present.

For example, a man offered his dream job says, "no" to a cross-country move. Why? In terms of seasonal time, his children are sophomores and seniors in high school. Regarding redemptive time, his wife thrives in Christ among rooted friends and a meaningful church.

Six years later, the kids have graduated. The man and his wife, say "yes" to a similar invitation. A time-eaten man couldn't delay for his kid's season or his wife's connection to redemptive time. He'd only see his daily time diminishing his life. And by the phrase, "his life" he'd only mean his job.

A wiser man recognizes that the life he'd miss out on includes the people he loves, the place he inhabits, the person he is, and the God who is with him.

Or consider Job's friends. They related to his suffering as if it were a time to build up, plant, heal, and speak, as if Job were in a theological discussion or accountability group. What Job's friends discerned at first but forgot was Job's season—a time of death, mourning, silence, losing, and enduring. It is a wise thing to be sad about sad things. Such tears are no waste of time.

The time-eater looks at wisdom's time-layers and grows impatient.

- *Daily time* with its four portions slows me down and seems boring. I've got more than I can do already and I'm already behind.

- *Seasonal time* doesn't impact me. I've got air-conditioned summers, heated winters, and fruit all year round, regardless of whether they are in season. I don't notice anymore. No delight or disquiet should altar my schedule or slow me down. Time is wasting.

- *Redemptive time* seems old, antique, stale, irrelevant to life as it is now. What Jesus did all those years ago seems distant and empty. All I have is me and this one life.

When we're "time-sick" like this:

- *We become season jumpers:* We naively try to skip the season we're in by impatiently prizing a future one. Like young lovers acting as if they're six years married in their first six weeks. Or the first day on the new job expecting to match and outshine a fifteen-year employee. Or appropriately grieving like Job and your friends skip ahead.
- *Or we become season clingers:* We foolishly try to hold off our emerging season by stubbornly prizing a past one. A boy grew up playing piano on Sunday mornings for a small church. Now college age, he's dating a woman from another town and seeking a job. "How could you leave us?" A parent or pastor says. "If you go, what'll happen to our worship of God? We've got no one else to play piano like you."

Season jumpers believe their best days are ahead of them. *Season clingers* believe their best days are behind them.

Both reveal their time-eaten struggle to believe that God is alive, present, capable and full of steadfast love, *right now*. Both feel more agitated than attentive, more harried than held, more listless than loved.

Moreover, when we're time sick, we thin our lives by untethering ourselves from redemptive time. We resist season jumping and clinging because this moment is all we have. We're *season erasers*. There's no past, no future, nothing beyond me. This moment and myself, is the only thing I have.

Time Reveals God's Steadfast Love

But what about the sun, moon, and stars and all the God-given skylight time-keepers abounding all around you?

> Give thanks to the LORD, for he is good ...
> to him who made the great lights,
>   for his steadfast love endures forever;
> the sun to rule over the day,
>   for his steadfast love endures forever;
> the moon and stars to rule over the night,
>   for his steadfast love endures forever (Ps. 136:1, 7-9).

And what about God's steadfast love in your past? The time-eater pictures our lives with no history, as if all has been consumed and is meaningless.

But in wisdom's house each person tells story after gleaming story, of who we once were, and how God was with us.

> It is he who remembered us in our low estate,
>   for his steadfast love endures forever;
> and rescued us from our foes,
>   for his steadfast love endures forever (Ps. 136:23-24).

The time-eater pictures our present moment as scarce, desperate and barren. But each person in wisdom's house tells a different story of

> he who gives food to all flesh,
>   for his steadfast love endures forever (Ps. 136:25).

The time-eater sculpture renders people and places as interruptions to our schedules.

But wisdom's house is full of folks rooted in a place. They arrive from "the east and from the west, from the north and from the south" (Ps. 107:3). They cheer for each other as each one has their own story to tell.

Some are desert dwellers. Others are sailors. There are farmers here side by side with city goers. The poor and the rich enjoy the same banqueted table. Fools who'd made a mess of life and prisoners whose lives were taken from war. All these and more. One by one, they stand to sing a song or tell the redemptive story of their lives.

And after each one's song and each one's telling, the whole listening company erupts with hilarity and grace, slaps on the back, and cheers all around. Arm in arm, together, they sing and shout and chant.

> Oh give thanks to the Lord, for he is good,
> for his steadfast love endures forever!
> Let the redeemed of the Lord say so (Ps. 107:1-2).

Imagine now, you're in a Bible study, quoting the Apostle Paul who urges us to "make the best use of the time" (Col. 4:5).

If we read "make the best use of the time," through the lens of time-eaten assumptions, we'll only renew our efforts to thin our souls by focusing upon the most efficient management of minutes, so we can minimize as many creation time interruptions as possible, by the effective use of untethered speed so we can produce more things, more famously as fast as possible for God.

But if we read, "make the best use of the time," from wisdom's time-enchanted point of view, we'll notice that Paul anchors his statement about time as an outworking of a wiser life.

> *Walk in wisdom* toward outsiders, *making the best use of the time* (Col. 4:5).

By now, we're beginning to understand the freight Paul is hauling when he uses the biblical word "wisdom." By now we know that wisdom, as with "Enchantment, isn't concerned" with a merely "scientific description of the world but with beholding the sacred meaning of the world."[111]

And what is the sacred meaning of the world but to recognize again the redemptive time in which you and I live?

In Jesus, time has waited long enough. God sends forth His Son (Gal. 4:4).

Time is then fulfilled. Jesus begins to preach (Mark 1:14-15).

They want to arrest Jesus. His hour has not yet come (John 7:30).

But then the Passover and Jesus announces, "my time is at hand" (Matt. 26:18)

Jesus is betrayed. His hour has come (Mark 14:41).

They crucify Him.

The third hour they spill His blood.

The sixth hour the sun and the afternoon quit.

The ninth hour Jesus breathes His last (Mark 15:25-39)

But then …

On the first day of the week, in the early morning, while it was still dark, the stone no longer closed the tomb.

The time-eater is dead.

The One who created time has killed it.

The One who gave us the gift of time has secured that gift.

This One who is greater than Solomon.

He's alive I tell you.

He's alive.

And the cross on which He died is wisdom's herald.

All the naive ways we used time to rob others' tears.

All the foolish ways we used time to rob others' individuality.

All the scoffing ways we used time to rob others of their dignity.

All the broken apart ways we used time to rob others of their joy.

Paid for.

Paid for in full.

And all of us who had our tears, individuality, dignity and joy, stolen?

We have an advocate. A defender.

* * *

Where is the one who is wise? …Where is the debater of this age? Hasn't God made the world's wisdom foolish? … For the Jews ask for signs and the Greeks seek wisdom, but we preach Christ crucified … the power of God and the wisdom of God, because God's foolishness is wiser than human wisdom, and God's weakness is stronger than human strength (1 Cor. 1:20-25, CSB).

10

Your Youth, Gray Hairs & Old Age

Remembering that you are going to die is the best way I know to avoid the trap of thinking you have something to lose. You are already naked. There is no reason not to follow your heart.[112]

The Natural is a favorite movie of mine. In it, a once-in-a-generation baseball player makes foolish choices in his youth and forfeits the life he dreamt of. Midlife, or what some have called "our second journey,"[113] affords the ballplayer a second chance.

A wise friend says to him.

> We have two lives, Roy: the life we learn with and the life we live with after that. Suffering is what brings us toward happiness ... It teaches us to want the right things.[114]

The story echoes two wiser truths. Our lives have seasons (The life we learn with and live with after that). Our lives encounter the menu of loves (It teaches us to want the right things).

But the movie and the novel it's based on present different responses. In one, Roy repeats his youthful errors. He and his loved ones suffer in midlife because earlier mistakes failed to prompt correction. In the other, Roy's response brings him to mature and contented old age.

Two paths emerge for a life lived.

The Wise Binder of Life

Biblical sages supply students an empty binder titled "Your Life and The Steadfast Love of God." They fill this binder with blank paper and section it with five labeled dividers, identifying the five core stories of our lives.

Our Birth
Our Youth
Our Gray Hairs
Our Old Age[115]
Our Death

Wisdom also provides a span of time in which students will live their five core stories.

The years of our life are seventy, or even by reason of strength eighty (Ps. 90:10).[116]

At fifty-nine, storyteller Walt Wangerin reflected on those who outlived the lifespan this wisdom verse suggests.

> It would be foolish to demand those extra years, and perilous to depend upon them. I depend upon the promises of my redeemer Jesus.[117]

Walt died at seventy-seven.[118]

Though some of us have "extra years," and others, like our Lord Jesus, painfully die too soon, most of us will say with the Psalmist. "I have been young, and now I am old" (Ps. 37:25).

Consequently, the wise fortify their students with a prayer.

Teach us to number our days that we may get a heart of wisdom (Ps. 90:12; 39:4).

Our earthly lives aren't time-eaten but God-inhabited (teach us). Our earthly lives begin and end (to number our days). With this knowledge, the menu of loves emerges. What will we most relish and reach for with our lives? The wisdom of God reshaping all we think, imagine, feel and do (that we may get a heart of wisdom).

The Questions of Life in our Youth

When I was a boy, a children's song asked, "Who are the people in your neighborhood?"[119]

As a help to kids, the song perhaps unwittingly echoed the biblical truth that when God created us, He gave each of us:

a thing to do,
a people to love,
a place to be,
a time to live,
and a plan to make.[120]

These five love tokens reveal life's recurring questions (and resemble wisdom's decision-making questions from our earlier chapter).

What am I going to do? (vocation, money, skill, enjoyment)
Who will I do this with? (relationships, friendship, singleness, marriage, sex, family)
Where will I live? (location)
When will it happen? (season and pace)
How will I go about it? (plan)

For most people,[121] we first answer these core questions in our youth, fresh with dew, carefree, and the sun rising (Eccles. 11:10; Ps. 110:3). We're energized and strong (Job. 33:25; Prov. 20:29), tasting wonder in a season of firsts.[122]

Wiser adults join us in our dreaming, ask good questions, offer stories and patient advice that doesn't shut us down but opens our eyes to positives and negatives we'd overlook if left to ourselves.

But naive, foolish, broken-apart, time-eaten adults turn these questions back on us, either with the urgent hounding expectation that we figure it out, or the absence of good questions because it's all fine, and whatever we want is happy, and it will all work out.

All adults see our possibilities. They dream again (Ps. 144:12). They share their dreams for us and cast them as possible futures. But sometimes adults use our youth to grasp what they once had but lost or never had but wanted. Growing up among adults with wisdom deficits is hard.

Mockingbirds
This is especially true when we're young, when we're like mockingbirds, trying on other people's voices. We are a "thief of other sounds,"[123] which is wise at first. Imitation is our best way of learning.

Imitation bodes well for us if we've grown up in the company of the wise. The voices we've thieved, pretended with and tried on, are wise too.

But growing up in a house of naivete or foolishness, among those who scoff or are broken apart, the voices we've thieved and tried on are unwise and amateur at love. By the time we rightly try our own voice, we do so as those little acquainted with wiser freedoms and horizons. We suffer unnecessary harm because of it.

But grace abounds. Childhood and youth describe the life we learn with. These are the years of mistake-making and being taught (Prov. 1:7), of sinning and being thoroughly forgiven (Prov. 25:7; 7:7; Ps. 119:9), of trying, succeeding, and being wholly celebrated, or trying, failing, and being helped up.

The One Greater than Solomon was twelve years old "in the temple sitting among the teachers, listening to them and asking them questions" (Luke 2:46). "The boy grew up and became strong, filled with wisdom, and God's grace was on him" (Luke 2:40 CSB).

Wisdom isn't delayed until we're older. Wisdom is meant to accrue by the time we are older.

But seeking wisdom in our youth doesn't change the fact that "To have a childhood means to live a thousand lives before the one."[124] We try on many faces and voices in search of wisdom's unique face and voice for us.

The Questions of Life in our Gray Hairs

If in our youth, we reach for many things, trying them on and dreaming about them, by the time we enter our gray-haired years, we must learn to let go of unwise things, unlearn them, and become a confessor regarding the wisdom we let go of or the folly we held onto in our youth.

Approaching midlife, some of our *best* memories reside within life's questions.

Remember what we did?!
How good those times were together!
Wouldn't it be great to go back there again?
It all happened at just the right time, didn't it?
How our plan came together was amazing!

We've tasted God's steadfast love. We don't want to let go of it.

But, entering our gray-haired years, we also pray things like:

Remember not the sins of my youth ...
according to your steadfast love remember me (Ps. 25:7).

What have I done?
I thought I knew who they were.

I don't ever want to go back there.
Why didn't I wait? Or *Why didn't I act when I had the chance?*
How did I not do that better? How did I choose so poorly?

There are some things we must now let go of if we hope to grow wiser of heart in our middle years. The first thing we must let go of is the picture of life we imagined when young in light of life as it is.

These contrasting pictures catch us off guard. At first we don't realize we're trying to make sense of these two pictures. What we do know is that we're looking at the condition of our family relationships, our job, the place we live, our aging parents, the church stuff we do, our bodily aches and a new question joins our list with intensifying feeling. The question, "why?"

We ask "why" either because what we dreamt in our youth never came to pass, or we got everything our younger selves wanted.

"Life keeps getting in the way of life," a young friend said. She'd hoped to be married, have children, a house, and a job she liked. She had all of this. But what a day requires of a woman who works, tends a yard, has a husband, family, friends, and three kids felt like a grind. "*Why* did I want this?" "*Why* am I doing this?"

Another friend thought he would have arrived by now.

> When I was younger I thought life would bring me to a clear and clean path. That by now I wouldn't still wrestle with the same questions. The path I'm on feels like a maze that leads to a cul-de-sac. Am I actually getting somewhere? What I thought I solved earlier seems to become a riddle again when set against these new circumstances I'm facing now that I'm older.

Yet, leaving our youth and entering our gray-haired years also has newfound opportunities. A man in his mid-thirties was offered a job his twenty-year-old self couldn't have had but dreamed of having. His older self gets to do what it took being older to have the chance at it.

He might also experience a freedom he didn't expect.

"I can't believe I'm saying this. I'm saying 'no' to this job."

I'd known this man many years. He was at ease now, a long way from the jittery man of his youth.

"It makes sense," I said. "You have a lot of data now. You aren't a kid anymore. You know things. You're realizing the difference between the voices you imitated and tried on, and the voice of a maturing you."

"That sounds freeing," he said.

"I think so too," I said. "You're less time-eaten. You have a freedom now that your younger self didn't. The freedom to say 'no' to something you once wanted. The freedom to know that you can have a good life without it. The freedom to admit that some things our younger selves wanted grew out of lying to ourselves. It would have crushed us if we got them."

Midlife Change

At forty (Acts 7:23), Moses grew less enamored with the wisdom he grew up with and more curious about the wisdom of God expressed among the people of Israel (Acts 7:22). He began to change his mind about his money, fame, and power while growing more attuned to his people's oppression. But choosing this wiser version of his God-given voice cost him.

First, unlearning the scripts of amateur love assumed in his youth will invite his family, friends, and co-workers to change. Moses wants to turn on a different light, and not everyone likes it. Some respond with anger. Moses' adoptive father disowns him and tries to kill him.

Second, none of us perfectly transition to a wiser version of our own voice. Moses' hair is grayer, his vision wiser, but he still trusts youthful tools.

> his own physical strength
> his own impatient sense of timing
> his own reactive anger
> isolating himself and going it alone
> access that only his wealth and power can secure
> his naive assumption that all will approve and applaud him

But Moses doesn't yet understand that the wiser way of life God has in mind will take four more decades. Sometimes we must enter the season of old age before we can fulfill a purpose our younger self couldn't imagine and our midlife self wasn't yet skilled for.

An opposite and more cautionary path beckons our attention with King David.

A younger and wiser David is sent a prophet to anoint him king. A midlife David is sent a prophet to confront him with his sin. David died when he was seventy (2 Sam. 5:4-5).

The grace of God never quit on David, and David, by grace, repents and never quits on God. But the damage was done. No one could have imagined David's sinful turn when they envisioned the wise and younger self, the one who faced Goliath with unwavering faith.

> Sometimes we hold onto what we ought to have let go of.
> Other times we let go of what we ought to have held onto.

I've Never Been Me

I spoke to a young man beginning his gray-haired years. A naive myth began to capture his imagination.

"I've never been my true self," he said, "Now I finally get to be me."

"What if you are 'the you' you've always been?" I asked. "When younger, you made the choices the younger you would make. Now you're not young anymore. You know what parts of your job you like and don't. You know to start a marriage and family takes one kind of skill set, but to deepen in a marriage with a family invites another set of skills. And some things are beyond your control, like your parents' health or the choices of your young adult children. What if you don't have a lost self to recover? What if you've always been you but you're older now, and you get to learn an older you's vision and skills?"

My friend didn't welcome this message.

In the end, to be the "him he'd never been," he traded in his wife and his car for new ones. He left his ministry and its people for new ones. He has a better, newer house, now too. He is unrecognizable to his wife, children, and those who loved and served with him when he was younger and wiser. He wrecked in his middle years what his younger self had the wisdom to cultivate.

The wise lament this. They teach such lament in a parable for their students.

> Better was a poor and wise youth than an old and foolish king who no longer knew how to take advice (Eccles. 4:13).

As I write, my culture's movies and books for middle-aged people forego wisdom's other important questions by focusing almost exclusively on ending a marriage, traveling to Italy or on some "adventure" to become one's true self and finally find a better romantic partner. Sex and romance are prized as the pre-eminent wisdom question of midlife. Our culture's craving on the menu of loves reveals itself, offering few stories capable of enabling a midlife person to navigate the fuller questions necessary for a wiser life.

In contrast, wisdom not only tells midlife stories about the one who "forsakes the companion of her youth and forgets the covenant of her God" (Prov. 2:16-17), but it also tells stories about many others like Paul[125] or Mary the mother of Jesus, and how these single and celibate people flourished amid midlife changes and choices.

Consider Anna. In her twenties, Anna is a woman of grief, wondering if her life can ever be happy again. By her middle years, Anna the widow is a prophetess. Was this a different life than her younger self dreamed? Or a thread always there in her youth but realized within the night light of her darkest sorrows?

Her younger self could never have imagined the old and wise woman she became. She blesses an entire nation, beholds Jesus face to face, and bears witness to God's promises in history. To this day, wisdom still tells Anna's story (Luke 2:36-38).

As the African Bishop, Augustine, entered his gray-haired years, he began to retrace his life. He wanted to interpret every difficult thing, every way he had sinned and been sinned against, not as if he'd never been who he was, but as if he'd always been him, just younger, and less wise or more vulnerable.

He writes his *Confessions*, as a "theography"[126] not merely an autobiography. In midlife, he pauses to ponder the path of his feet by looking back and retelling the story of each scene of his life as if he and his world weren't alone but undergirded by the presence and persistence of God's steadfast love.

In midlife, the wise become confessors. They retrace their youth looking for God's steadfast love. They begin to unlearn and let go so they can better hold onto the mattering things.

Jesus hasn't quit on us. There is hope, even for a man or woman like David, who abandoned in older age the wisdom his younger self cherished. But not the hope a person can afford to take for granted, for we live only seventy years and, by strength, eighty.

Old Age
As I write, a ninety-one-year-old has been seeking me out between services on Sunday mornings. Death is on his mind. He's been retracing his life; seeking to forgive, be forgiven, and cherish cherished things.

"I'm ready now to go home to see my Lord." His wife nods yes. They hold hands.

"Did you feel this readiness to die when you were my age?" I asked.

"Definitely not," he says. "I couldn't have spoken like this then. I was too cluttered up. My career. The kids. I would have been afraid to talk like this back then."

I asked if they'd share with our "Wisdom for middle-age" group.

He said "yes" immediately. When the time came, he spoke of how his middle-years crowded out love for God and for people.

"But Christ can change you," he said. "You can love as an old man, in a way that you didn't even understand when you were younger."

But when I'd asked them to speak, she said, "no" immediately. "I've nothing to share. My middle age was so heartbreaking. I wouldn't wish it on anybody."

We had several conversations in the days ahead. I finally risked a question.

"How did you get from no hope in your midlife to such deep hope now? What if someone in their middle years feels exactly as you did then? Something got you through it. Knowing what that something is might help someone who feels they wouldn't wish their current life on anybody."

She agreed. When the time came, she spoke of the grace of God given through His Word and promises, through a few dear friends, a counselor, and many tears.

They both shared of course about how physical frailties form a more prominent part of their prayer lives now (Ps. 71:9). He wears hearing aids. She has arthritis.

They mentioned too, how sometimes, with so many of their family and friends gone now, they can feel lonely. "I consider the days of old, the years long ago," the Psalmist says (Ps. 77:5), and by now most people we talk to weren't there and didn't see what we saw. Their grown children and grandchildren don't always understand and yet, how can they?

But mostly, her husband spoke of being changed by love.

She spoke of being changed by hope.

Both spoke of these changes as acts of faith in Jesus who'd lavished His grace upon them.

The wise picture the aged as fruit-bearing people. The Lord roots them, nourishes them, tends them.

> They still bear fruit in old age;
> they are ever full of sap and green,
> to declare that the LORD is upright;
> he is my rock, and there is no unrighteousness in him
> (Ps. 92:14-15).

Passing On the Mattering Things

I've known such old ones full of sap and green.

"Zack, you're just a young pup, you know that don't you?"

I was forty-nine. Talking like my life's work had passed me by.

The one saying this to me was eighty-seven and full of life.[127]

"Really," he said. "If the good Lord gives you life, you have at least three more full adventures ahead of you from start to finish. Hard things? Yes. But good things, too. People you've not met yet. Good experiences with God and for God you couldn't yet envision."

He'd traveled the world and preached the gospel in stadiums. He'd spoken of Jesus among the famous and in huts among the poor. He'd written books and led powerful movements of grace, that I and my generation little remember.

But in his fifties, one of his sons died too young. Gradually, our mentor left speaking to crowds in favor of listening to individuals. He began to learn how to paint and to write poems as a way of helping him more wisely grow attentive to God's world and to God's work within the people in front of him.

And now, because of that risky shift decades earlier within his gray-haired years, I (along with so many others) were being helped. In his old age, he was passing on the mattering things (as well as skilled paintings and poems his younger self could scarcely have imagined).

He would have done great good if he continued the shape of his youthful vocation through his midlife years. Yet I (and countless other young leaders globally) would likely never have met him.

As he neared ninety, in our last formal gathering of an annual mentoring community, he sat with all of us, his white hair whispy and his blue eyes shining fire within them. He said, "If you find yourself old like me someday, remember this moment. When we age our world shrinks. We aren't asked to do things like we once were. Our bodies can't sustain what they once did. Many of our closest friends have passed on. We lose our sense of purpose or sense of contribution regarding Jesus and His kingdom in the world. But you are my friends. You still have invitations, energy, purpose, opportunity. I learn from you. You keep me aware of the world and of our Lord's work within it. I hope I have offered good to you over these years, but I want you to know the good you've given me. When you are old, and I'm no longer here, remember how I needed younger friends, with whom I could continue to grow in my faith. You too will need such friends. God is happy to give them to you. Don't shrink your life. Give it away in friendship and lean upon such friendship."

At ninety-three, sitting on a porch overlooking Grandfather Mountain, a smaller few of us sat with him. It was mountain evening cold. He wore a blanket. We sat by a fire.

He asked, "What is our Lord doing in your life these days to keep the fire of His love within you warm and alive?"

He listened as each of us found words and answers.

One of us asked him the same question. He told us how he'd just called a mentor who is 102 years old. "What do I need to know to follow Jesus in my nineties?"

I was struck by how even in old age, he was humbling himself, curious and teachable toward the basic questions he'd navigated since his youth. What will I do? Who will I do it with? Where will I do it? When will it come to pass? Why am I doing it?

The centenarian had answered my ninety-three-year-old friend. "Trust God with your limits. Find the humor in things especially in who you are now compared to who you once were. Keep doing the good things God gives you, however small."

When I was younger, perhaps I thought of the deathbed, and all its miserable riot in our bodies, as death's victory. As if our loved ones were breathing their last as a sign that the grim reaper had come for them.

The wise know better. Breathing our last is death mustering its last stand. It isn't the grim reaper who comes for us, but the One Greater than Solomon, the One through whom God's steadfast love was given before we were born. The One through whom we've always been held. What we see in the last miserable moment is death losing its grip. Our last enemy is dying right before our eyes. And the Christ in whom we have believed, walks powerfully toward us. He peels death's last grip from us. He gathers us into His arms. He stands us up, looks into the eyes of who he made us to be. He speaks our name. The wonder of it. Our name spoken on the lips of divine love.

No love on the menu of your life can compare.

Time	Purpose	Life skill	Identity
Your Pre-birth	Held by the one thing	trusting	beloved of God
Your Birth	Adjusting to everything	surviving and learning	child
Your Youth	Reaching out for many things	trying	dreamer
Your Gray Hairs	Letting go of unwise things	unlearning	confessor
Your Old Age	Passing on the mattering things	befriending	mentor
Your Earthly Death	Holding on to the one thing	conquering our last enemy	lover of God

11

Postscript

As we close our book together, I feel like one at a support group, needing to confess.

"Hi," I say. "My name is Zack."

You say, "Hi, Zack."

I say, "I'm a love-a-holic. I've misused and mishandled love. I've been naive, a fool, tempted to scoff. I've hurt myself. I've hurt others and I'm worn out with it all. I grew up in wrecked homes." (I catch myself. I'm on the verge of talking about others rather than owning my own problems).

"But I'm the worst of us," I continue. "I'm the pastor in the family—the professional god-talker. I too am a divorced man, remarried. I've spoken for God and sometimes known little of the good I've tried to talk about. Wise love is hard enough to find in this world, but the heartache worsens when god-talkers like me misname God in the midst of it all."

I pause. In my mind, I hear the gentle voices of wiser ones who know me best. "You're being too hard on yourself," they tell me. "Remember, this is no all-or-nothing story."

So, I look up and try to talk to you again.

"When I grew up, we didn't know anything about what the Bible calls wisdom or that Jesus was wise with love. Jesus was a statue in a sanctuary. He cared more about your being good enough rather than what you laughed or cried about in your deep soul when no one else was around. Now I look back and I know myself to be what songwriter John Foreman called, an "Amateur Lover."[128]

(I'm feeling hesitant now; afraid I'm making no sense. A memory from speech basics comes to mind. "Define what you mean," it says to me. So, I look out at you and search for definition).

"As amateurs, we possess raw talent, solid potential and genuine heart. But at some point, if we want to grow, we must start the humbling work of measuring ourselves by the masters of the craft, rather than its novices. If any of us is going to find a better life, we have to finally put down our pride, let go of the hacks at love we've called wise, and courageously embrace the discomfort of health that following a master guide will require."

I pause searching for words.

"When my oldest son and I gave ourselves to all that training to get our black belt, the master told us we were now ready to begin. It's like that for you and for me right now. We've talked all about wisdom in these pages. But we haven't arrived. Far from it. We've merely trained enough in the categories we'll need to finally get started."

I look down now. I'm sounding like a preacher and I know it. So, I clear my throat. I look back up and out at each of you. It's like I am staring at a birthday candle, finally getting to the point and ready to make a wish.

"My Higher Power is Jesus as the Bible reveals Him," I say.

"His love isn't amateur and ours no longer has to be."

Endnotes

1. Esther de Waal, "A Prayer of Columba," *The Celtic Way of Prayer* (The Crown Publishing Group. Kindle Edition), 6-7.

2. Jamin Roller, "Wisdom and Wonder: A Sermon" (January 23, 2022). https://citizenschurch.com/resources/sermon/753

3. Aristotle located his helpful discussion on wisdom with the intellectual virtues of thinking well and knowledgeably so as to discern and decide in favor of those honorable things conducive to a happy life. For a summary of Aristotle and wisdom see Michael C. Legaspi and Ryan Hanley, "Wisdom and Tradition: Aristotle" (April 6, 2010), The Center for Practical Wisdom, https://wisdomcenter.uchicago.edu/news/discussions/wisdom-and-tradition-aristotle

4. Daniel J. Ebert IV, *Wisdom Christology: How Jesus Becomes God's Wisdom for Us* (Phillipsburg, New Jersey: P&R Publishing 2011), 179.

5. Referring to Lady Wisdom personified in Proverbs 8, Daniel J. Ebert IV notes important foreshadowing connections but not a "one-to-one" correspondence to Jesus. "Like the ancient literary figure of Wisdom, Jesus reveals God and his ways. But in his full identity as the divine Son, and consequently in his ability to reveal God, Jesus far surpasses all other religious figures." *Wisdom Christology: How Jesus Becomes God's Wisdom For Us* (P&R Publishing, 2011), 47.

6. E.E. Cummings, "I Thank you God for Most This Amazing," This poem was originally published in *Xaipe* (New York: Oxford University Press 1950), reissued in 2004 by Liveright, an imprint of W.W. Norton & Company.

7. Timothy and Kathy Keller, *God's Wisdom for Navigating Life: A Year of Daily Devotions in the Book of Proverbs* (New York: Penguin Random House 2017), xii.

8. Martin Shaw, *Smokehole: Looking to the Wild in the Time of the Spyglass* (London, UK: Chelsea Green Publishing 2021), 18.

9. C. S. Lewis, "Meditation in a Tool Shed," in *God in the Dock* (Grand Rapids, Michigan: Eerdmans 1970), 212-215.

10. Norton Juster, *The Phantom Tollbooth* (New York: Yearling 1989), 77.

11. "Wisdom has on the whole not had an easy time in recent centuries in the West. It has often been associated with old people, the premodern, tradition, and conservatism in a culture of youth, modernization, innovation, and risky exploration." David F. Ford, *Christian Wisdom: Desiring God and Learning in Love*, Cambridge Studies in Christian Doctrine (Cambridge: Cambridge University Press 2007), 1.

12. "You are no doubt all aware that the New Testament minister corresponds not at all to the Old Testament priest, but in important respects to the Old Testament prophet." John Broadus, *Lectures on the History of Preaching* (New York: Sheldon & Company 1876), 10. For Broadus, Ecclesiastes might introduce preachers to a "certain class of sermons," but says nothing more and prefers the prophetic paradigm for preachers. Likewise, Edwin Dargin looks to Proverbs and the preacher of Ecclesiastes for "hints" regarding "the preparation of ... religious teachers," but goes no further, instead prioritizing the prophet, *The Art of Preaching*, 20.

13. Also see, Paul: "Him we proclaim, warning everyone and teaching everyone with all wisdom, that we may present everyone mature in Christ" (Col. 1:28).

14. "Therefore, that faith may find in Christ a solid ground of salvation, and so rest in him, we must set out with this principle, that the office which he received from the Father consists of three parts. For he was appointed both Prophet, King, and Priest." John Calvin, *Institutes*, chapter 15.

15. "Whereas the prophetic aspect of Jesus' teaching usually receives its due recognition, there is a tendency to overlook and underestimate the role of Jesus as a sage." Robert H. Stein, The Method and Message of Jesus' Teachings (Philadelphia: Westminster Press 1978), 2. "We forget the saying of Jeremiah: 'The law shall not perish from the priest, nor counsel from the wise, nor the word from the prophet' (Jer. 18:18). We find these— all these styles—in Christ." Amos N. Wilder, T*he Language of the Gospel: Early Christian Rhetoric* (New York: Harper & Row 1964), 86.

16. On this point and the next, I give thanks to Jerram Barrs who introduced many of us to a marvelous exception to this experience. See his *Heart of Evangelism* or *Being Human*.

17. Augustine, *Enchiridion on Faith, Hope and Love*, trans. J. B. Shaw (Washington, D.C.: Regnery Publishing Inc. 1996), 1-2.

18. E.g., 1, 14, 37, 49, 73, 91, 112, 119, and 128.

19. See for example, J. De Waal Dryden, *A Hermeneutic of Wisdom: Recovering the Formative Agency of Scripture* (Grand Rapids, MI: Baker Academic, 2018).

20. Wisdom's house imitates God's house "They feast in the abundance of your house, and you give them drink from the river of your delights. For with you is the fountain of life; in your light do we see light." (Ps. 36:8-9).

21. By "loud," the wise aren't talking about decibals. Some people have louder natural voices than others. In the Scriptures, two things are described in positive terms as loud: praise and lament. By "loud," the wise mean talk full of boasting, unfiltered, constantly heralding itself. 2 Peter 2:18-19; Jude 1:16.

22. "Seductive" means smooth, attractive, feels good, appealing, offers what you want. For example, notice Proverbs 7. This sexual situation is loud and seductive.

23. Walker Percy, *The MovieGoer* (London: Methuen Publishing Ltd 2004)

24. Taika Waititi, *Hunt for the Wilderpeople* (2016), https://www.scripts.com/script-pdf/10388, 14-15.

25. John Donne, "Batter My Heart O Three Person'd God".

26. Biblical sages will quote and affirm true things said by people who didn't believe in the God of Israel. See Tremper Longman III, *Proverbs*, Baker Commentary on the Old Testament Wisdom and Psalms (Grand Rapids, MI: Baker Academic 2006), 57-58. Notice how the Apostle Paul follows this wisdom way (Acts 17:28, Titus 1:12, 1 Cor. 15:33)

27. Norton Juster and Lenoard Baskin, *Alberic the Wise* (Saxonville, Massachusetts: Picture Book Studio 1992), 13.

28. Zack Eswine, "Apologetic Communication: How Someone Who Isn't a Christian is Meant to Experience Someone Who Is," *Firstfruits of a New Creation: Essays Honoring Jerram Barrs* (Oklahoma City, OK: White Blackbird Books 2019), 249.

29. Sheryl Paul, *The Wisdom of Anxiety: How Worry and Intrusive Thoughts are Gifts to Help You Heal* (Boulder, CO: Sounds True 2019), Kindle, location 801 of 3996.

30. The biblical equivalent of this fictional tale is Samson with Delilah. We'll come back to this in chapter three.

31. Raymond C. Ortlund Jr., *Proverbs: The Wisdom that Works,* in Preaching the Word Series, Ed., R. Kent Hughes (Wheaton, Illinois: Crossway Books 2012), 21-22.

32. Edward J. Carnell, T*he Kingdom of Love and the Pride of Life* (Oregon: Wipf & Stock 2007), 16.

33. Ibid., 19-20.

Endnotes

34. Sor Juana Inés de la Cruz "You Foolish Men," https://poets.org/poem/you-foolish-men

35. "The fool says in his heart, "There is no God." (Ps. 14:1). Believing in God a foolish heart applies this verse to others, not realizing that by refusing wise advice, and choosing slowness to listen, quickness to speak, and quickness to vent anger, they act as if God is neither present nor wise.

36. Henry Cloud, *Necessary Endings: The Employees, Businesses, and Relationships that All of us Have to Give Up in Order to Move Forward* (New York: Harper Business 2010), 128, 133.

37. Likewise, consider a businessman who "says to himself, I will, I will, I will, I will." "Fool," God says. Tonight, you die (Luke 12:13-21; see Prov. 18:1-2).

38. For a parable regarding how fool's demand wisdom's surrender see Kahlil Gibran, "The Wise King," Poetry Foundation https://www.poetryfoundation.org/poems/58702/the-wise-king

39. This insight noting naivete and folly both grow sluggardly comes from Melissa McKinney, Sage Leaders Cohort, Fall 2023.

40. Dan B. Allender and Tremper Longman III, *Bold Love* (Colorado: NavPress 1992), Location 2974 loving a fool

41. Nathan Eswine, "Villain" *Freeze Tag: Tendencies* (2020).

42. Amy Carmichael, *Gold By Moonlight: Sensitive Lessons from a Walk with Pain*, Chapter Three "The Ravine" (Kindle Edition, Location 258 of 2625).

43. Daniel Nayeri, *Everything Sad Is Untrue* (New York: Levine Querido 2020), 298-299 Kindle Edition.

44. Flannery O'Connor, "A Good Man is Hard to Find," in *The Complete Stories* (New York: Farrar, Straus and Giroux 1971), 132. Similarly, "I got to the point of feeling a sort of secret abnormal, despicable enjoyment in returning home ... acutely conscious that that day I had committed a loathsome action ... turned into a

sort of shameful accursed sweetness ... a positive real enjoyment" Dostoevsky, *Notes from the Underground*, 212.

45. Carrie Pilby movie script https://www.scripts.com/script-pdf/5105

46. Notice the parallelism of the Hebrew poetry, which presents scoffer as a synonym for wicked.

47. Dr. Henry Cloud, *Necessary Endings* (New York: HarperCollins 2011), 143 Kindle Edition.

48. Bruce Springsteen, "Devils and Dust," in *Devils and Dust* (2005).

49. For another example of how pain and misery tempt us to scoff see 1 Samuel 30:7. David and his men all face the same excruciating mental pain. In his agony, David chooses God's wisdom as the path forward while his men are tempted to choose misusing power and murder as the best way forward.

50. When others criticize us our "spirit faints" within us (Ps. 142:3; 143:4). A relentless barrage of slanders can "break" our spirit (Prov. 15:4).

51. C.S. Lewis, *The Problem of Pain* (Nashville, TN: Zondervan 2011)

52. Tim Burton, "James," in *The Melancholy Death of Oyster Boy & Other Stories* (New York: William Morrow and Company 1997), 70-71.

53. I've added "bodyaches," to Ron Rolheiser's regular talk about "headaches and heartaches," to describe those things that make life difficult and keep us from our love relationship with God. Rolheiser implies "bodyaches" when he says: "It's hard to pray when we suffer from the kind of headaches and heartaches that cannot be eased by taking an aspirin." Ron Rolheiser, "Obstacles to Prayer," (March 9, 2003) https://ronrolheiser.com/obstacles-to-prayer/ see for example Psalm 35:13.

54. For more on the wisdom of proportionate grief see Zack Eswine, *Spurgeon's Sorrows: Realistic Hope for those who Suffer from Depression* (Ross-shire: Christian Focus 2014), 27-30.

55. Amy Carmichael, *Gold by Moonlight: Sensitive Lessons from a Walk with Pain*, Chapter Two, "The Dark Wood," (Kindle Location 139 of 2625).

56. Parker J. Palmer, *On the Brink of Everything: Grace, Gravity, & Getting Old* (Oakland: Berrett-Koehler Publishers 2018), 139 Kindle Edition.

57. Henri Nouwen, *The Wounded Healer: Ministry in Contemporary Society* (New York: Image Books/Doubleday, 1972).

58. Scientific research confirms and echoes this ancient teaching of the biblically wise. See for example, Bessel A van der Kolk, *The Body Keeps the Score: Brain, Mind and Body in the Healing of Trauma* (London: Penguin Books, 2015).

59. Zack Eswine, "What Anxiety Feels Like. Is There Hope?" Sage Christianity (August 10, 2021). https://www.sagechristianity.com/articles-essays/what-anxiety-feels-like-confessions-of-a-pastor?rq=eswine

60. Zack Eswine, "Care for the Sinner," in *The Imperfect Pastor: Discovering Joy in Our Limitations through a Daily Apprenticeship with Jesus* (Wheaton, Illinois: Crossway Books 2015), Chapter 13.

61. Zack Eswine, "Failure Need Not Be Final," Desiring God (September 17, 2022). https://www.desiringgod.org/articles/failure-need-not-be-final

62. This observation was prompted by a talk given by Valdir and Sileda Steuernagel, Resurgence Conference, September 2023, Campinus Brazil.

63. Rainer Maria Rilke, *Letters to a Young Poet*, (New York: W.W. Norton & Company, 1993), 42-43.

64. Ibid., 45.

65. Walker Percy, *Love in the Ruins: A Novel* (New York: Picador 1971), 6.

66. Josef Pieper, *Faith, Hope, Love* (San Francisco, CA: Ignatius Press, 2012), 170-174.

67. One Republic, Mosley Music Group and Interscope Records, *Native* "Counting Stars," (March 22, 2013), C.D.

68. See Augustine, *On Christian Doctrine*, I.27-28.

69. Gnōsis generally conveys the idea of an experiential knowledge (the product of experiencing by living). It easily lends itself to expressing relationships since they come from experiences. Further, since experiences provide the process of learning, gnōsis often stresses the process of knowing, rather than the outcome. Here Paul used the term in its full sense of real, personal knowing. It is not the product of deductive reasoning and, therefore, intellectual (oida). Richard R. Melick Jr., *Philippians, Colossians, Philemon*: The New American Commentary, Vol. 32 (Nashville, TN: Holman Reference 1991), 65.

70. '[I]n all insight', that is, into all types of situations involving practical conduct," P.T. O'Brien, *The Epistle to the Philippians: a commentary on the Greek text* (Eerdmans, 1991), 73.

71. The word "discern," has to do with "sapient knowledge," *Dictionary of Biblical Languages with Semantic Domains*: Greek (New Testament).

72. Erich Fromm, *The Art of Loving*, (Harper Perennial Modern Classics, 2019), 4.

73. Fromm, *The Art of Loving*, 1.

74. Fromm, *The Art of Loving*, 5. As an example of Fromm's point, I have masters and doctoral degrees. Though I trained for ministry, I've had only one class on wisdom which was a one-semester overview of the Bible's wisdom literature. I've never had a class on love. I did not know nor was I asked to think through

the Christian classics on love handed down through the centuries. Nor did I recognize this as a problem.

75. Exodus 34:6-7

76. Scholars note exposition of the Shema from Deuteronomy 6 in these verses. See Tremper Longman III, *Proverbs*, Baker Commentary on the Old Testament Wisdom and Psalms (Grand Rapids MI: Baker Academic 2006), 132.

77. Augustine, Sermon on 1 John 4:4-12, https://christianhistoryinstitute.org/study/module/augustine "Human actions can only be understood by their root in love. All kinds of actions might appear good without proceeding from the root of love. If you hold your peace, hold your peace out of love. If you cry out, cry out in love. If you correct someone, correct them out of love. If you spare them, spare them out of love. Let the root of love be in you: nothing can spring from it but good."

78. My retelling from John Cassian, *Conferences*, The Classics of Western Spirituality, transl., Colm Luibheid (New York: Paulist Press 1985), 65-66.

79. Discernment takes time, practice, and learning from mistakes (Heb. 5:14).

80. The Hebrew word in Proverbs 16:21 is בִּין, bin

81. "... his ways are past finding out," (Rom. 11:33; Eccles. 8:17; 11:5).

82. All a person's ways seem right to him, but the Lord weighs motives ... There is a way that seems right to a person, but its end is the way to death (Proverbs 16:2-3, 25, CSB). Until heaven, we "see things imperfectly, like puzzling reflections in a mirror ... partial and incomplete" (1 Cor. 13:12, NLT).

83. Mark Ryan made note of this in a Sage Leader's Cohort, Fall 2023, drawing upon Craig G. Bartholomew and Michael W. Goheen, *The Drama of Scripture: Finding our Place in the Biblical Story* (Grand Rapids, Michigan: Baker Academic 2014). Chapter 1: Creation, Chapter 2: Fall, Chapter 3: The King Chooses Israel,

Chapter 4: The Coming of the King, Chapter 5: Spreading the News of the King, Chapter 6: The Return of the King.

84. These images refer to washing and tending our clothes and our bodies.

85. Moses too chose this same approach of finding wise people to handle the dilemma that confronted them (Exod. 18:21)

86. "The one who accepts correction will be honored," (Prov. 13:18; 5:11-14; 12:1; 15:5).

87. See, "Trusting the Spirit's Appointed Means, Seeking the Spirit's Attendant Power, Bowing Before the Spirit's Mysteries, and Pursuing the Spirit's Fellowship," in Zack Eswine, *Kindled Fire: How the Methods of C.H. Spurgeon Can Help Your Preaching* (Ross-shire: Christian Focus 2006), 133-194). "Discern Devilish Spin," and "Cry Out for the Holy Spirit," in Zack Eswine, *Preaching to a Post-Everything World: Crafting Biblical Sermons That Connect with our Culture* (Grand Rapids, MI: Baker 2008), 231-259. See "Beholding God," and "Finding our Pace," Zack Eswine, *The Imperfect Pastor: Discovering Joy in our Limitations Through a Daily Apprenticeship with Jesus* (Wheaton Illinois: Crossway 2015), 151-168, 179.

88. We can mistakenly hear these words as denigrating serving and preferring preaching. What "isn't right" is widows uncared for and the ministry of the Word stalled. Both are equally commanded and commended. If the apostles stretch to do all the ministry of service and teaching both are hindered. But if the apostles free everyone to have a role to play, the full ministry of service and teaching can flourish.

89. Early Christian decision-makers often use phrases like these. "We thought it was better," (1 Thess. 3:1-2), or we "considered it necessary," (Phil. 2:25-26), "suitable," (1 Cor. 16:3-4), "right" (Acts 6:1-4) or "good to us" (Acts 15:18-28). See Garry Friesen and J. Robin Maxson, *Decision Making and the Will of God* (Sisters OR: Multnomah, 2009), 138-152.

90. It is prudent to remember the supernatural experience Paul once had, but didn't share with anyone for thirteen years, and then, only in a context that humbles him to his critics (2 Cor. 12).

91. Henri Nouwen, *Discernment: Reading the Signs of Daily Life* (New York: HarperCollins, 2013), 6.

92. Richard Beck, *Hunting Magic Eels: Recovering an Enchanted Faith in a Skeptical Age* (Minneapolis, MN: Broadleaf Books, 2021), 25.

93. Dallas Willard helpfully reframes our decision-making from the man who hid his talent, believing God harsh, to the dearly loved child and friend of God. He writes: "God is not a cosmic boss, foreman or autocrat, whose chief joy in relation to humans is ordering them around, taking pleasure in seeing them jump at his command and painstakingly noting any failures. Instead, we are to be God's friends (2 Chron 20:7; John 15:13-15) and fellow workers (1 Cor. 3:9 nasb)." Dallas Willard, *Hearing God: Developing a Conversational Relationship with God*, IVP Signature Collection (InterVarsity Press. Kindle Edition), 41.

94. Thomas à Kempis, *The Imitation of Christ* (Chicago: Moody Press 1958), 106-7.

95. "Love is designed to be our primary way of 'being with' others ... in this union of souls it is not right for one person to always tell the other what to do. And so it is in our union with God ... He does not delight in having to always explain what his will is; he enjoys it when we understand and act upon his will. Our highest calling and opportunity in life is to love him with all our being." Dallas Willard, *Hearing God*, 40.

96. Robert Henri, *The Art Spirit*, 85th Anniversary Edition (Cambridge, MA: Basic Books Edition 2007), 13-14.

97. Parts of this chapter published as Zack Eswine, "Dear Pastor ... When You Wonder How You'll Make it, Remember this," (June 18, 2023, Crossway) https://www.crossway.org/articles/dear-pastor-when-you-wonder-how-youll-make-it-remember-this/

98. Philip Larkin, "Aubade," in *Philip Larkin: Collected Poems*, ed., Anthony Thwaite (New York: Farrar, Straus and Giroux 2003), 190.

99. Charles Spurgeon, "The Sacred Love Token," A sermon in T*he Metropolitan Tabernacle Pulpit*, Vol. 21 (Ages Digital Library 1998), 610ff.

100. Ibid.

101. Justin Whitmel Earley, *Habits of the Household* (Grand Rapids, MI: Zondervan, November 9, 2021), 35 Kindle Edition.

102. Martin Luther, *Galatians Commentary*, 1:4 https://www.studylight.org/commentaries/eng/mlg/galatians-1.html

103. Richard Beck, *Hunting Magic Eels: Recovering an Enchanted Faith in a Skeptical Age* (Minneapolis, Minnesota: Broadleaf Books 2021), 32.

104. https://hyperallergic.com/432535/corpus-clock-stephen-hawking/. http://www.johnctaylor.com/the-chronophage/

105. Carl Honore, *In Praise of Slowness: Challenging the Cult of Speed* (San Francisco: Harper One, 2004), 3. Quoted in Andrew Root, *The Congregation in a Secular Age: Keeping Time Against the Speed of Modern Life* (Grand Rapids, MI: Baker Academic 2021), 46.

106. To explore more about wisdom and time see Zack Eswine, *Recovering Eden: The Gospel According to Ecclesiastes* (Phillipsburg, New Jersey: P&R Publishing 2014), 117-144.

107. Nathaniel Meyersohn, "A Major Shift at Starbucks is Changing It's Personality," CNN Fri July 19, 2024 https://www.cnn.com/2024/07/19/business/starbucks-mobile-orders-third-place/index.html

108. "There is no longer ... a sense that the created realm participates in a heavenly one. Eternity is shut out of time and now time is free to rev its engines ... To get time to speed up it had to have its meaning hollowed out, unhooked from divine consequence."

Andrew Root, *The Congregation in a Secular Age: Keeping Time Against the Speed of Modern Life* (Grand Rapids, MI: Baker Academic 2021), 47, 50.

109. To explore these themes further see Zack Eswine, *The Imperfect Pastor: Discovering Joy in our Limitations through a Daily Apprenticeship with Jesus* (Wheaton, Illinois: Crossway Books 2015), especially chapters 1, 10 & 11.

110. Henri Nouwen, *Turn My Mourning into Dancing: Finding Hope in Hard Times* (Nashville, Tennessee: W Publishing Group, 2001), Kindle Book location 475-476.

111. Beck, *Hunting Magic Eels*, 95.

112. Steve Jobs, "How to Live Before You Die," (Stanford University, June 2005). https://www.ted.com/talks/steve_jobs_how_to_live_before_you_die

113. Leighton Ford, *A Life of Listening: Discerning God's Voice and Discovering our Own, A Memoir* (Downers Grove, Illinois: Intervarsity Press 2019).

114. Bernard Malamud, *The Natural* (London: Vintage Classics 2002), 152. Also, https://www.imdb.com/title/tt0087781/quotes/

115. For examples of how wisdom describes these three seasons of age, notice verses such as: "Both the gray-haired and the aged are among us" (Job 15:10) or "the young men saw me and withdrew, and the aged rose and stood" (Job 29:8). "Now Elihu had waited to speak to Job because they were older than he" (Job. 32:4).

116. As I write, the average life span globally is 68.9 years for men and 73.9 years for women. In the United States, it's 79 years for women and 73 years for men WorldData.Info https://www.worlddata.info/lifeexpectancy.php#:~:text=Life%20expectancy%20for%20men%20and%20women&text=The%20world%20average%20age%20of,and%2073.9%20years%20for%20women.

117. Walter Wangerin Jr., *This Earthly Pilgrimage: Tales and Observations on the Way* (Grand Rapids, Michigan: Zondervan 2003), 12.

118. Foolish hearts balk at the funeral talk wiser ones will take to heart (Eccles. 7:3-4). Naivete affirms folly's aversion by rolling their eyes and giggling at this serious conversation. But the wise learn to ponder death as part of life (Eccles. 7:2), not morbidly, but purposefully as those anchored by the steadfast love of God and empowered to live.

119. For one iteration of the song see, Sesame Street, "Who are the People in Your Neighborhood?" https://www.youtube.com/watch?v=V2bbnlZwlGQ

120. To go deeper here see Zack Eswine, *The Imperfect Pastor.*

121. I say "most" because, for some, our youth is painfully fast-forwarded into old-age challenges. Our bodies do not work as we'd hoped. "We're blind from birth" (John 9:1-41). When broken open by His steadfast love, such persons become thriving old souls who teach wise love to us. I think of a wheelchaired man in our congregation. Since his youth, he has had to sit to get where he's going. His vocal cords work only with great effort. Yet, there he is, during a time of thanksgiving in a morning worship service, declaring out loud from his heart what he thanks God for. He is our teacher and friend. One day in the new kingdom, as fellow death conquerors, we'll run together within the sun and moon of our scarred Savior's light. We'll sit and laugh and talk about everything we couldn't say or understand back when we tried and all was not yet set right.

122. Paul Angone, *101 Secrets for Your Twenties* (Chicago Illinois: Moody Publishers 2013)

123. Mary Oliver, *Mockingbird*

124. Rainer Maria Rilke, *Letters on Life* (New York: The Modern Library 2006), 69.

125. Paul persecutes Christians as a "young man." In his gray-haired years, Jesus knocks Paul off his horse. A chunk of Paul's midlife is spent in significant quiet, resetting for his future calling. He stays away in Syria, Cilicia, and Arabia for fourteen years before he comes back and begins preaching in Jerusalem (Gal. 1:18; 2:1). When Paul writes his letter to Philemon around a.d. 62, he can say he is an "old man" (Phile. 1:9). Young Jewish Paul who used intellect and violence against Christians and berated Gentile people as unclean, now travels as a Christian to Gentile peoples. Midlife Paul has chosen a life so different that young Paul would have considered it blasphemous. What changed? Paul was met by Jesus. In contrast, Mary followed God from her youth. She is widowed and by midlife watches her son brutally killed. Through many dangers toils and snares Mary only grows deeper, truer and more faithful.

126. See the doctoral work of Dr. Davi C. Ribeiro-Lin, https://www.gordonconwell.edu/faculty/current/davi-ribeiro-lin/

127. For more of this mentor's wisdom see Leighton Ford, *A Life of Listening: Discerning God's Voice and Discovering our Own* (Downers Grove, Illinois: Intervarsity Press, 2019). Or *The Attentive Life: Discerning God's Presence in All Things* (Downers Grove, Illinois: Intervarsity Press, 2014).

128. Ibid.

Christian Focus Publications

Our mission statement
Staying Faithful

In dependence upon God we seek to impact the world through literature faithful to His infallible Word, the Bible. Our aim is to ensure that the Lord Jesus Christ is presented as the only hope to obtain forgiveness of sin, live a useful life and look forward to heaven with Him.

Our Books are published in four imprints:

CHRISTIAN FOCUS

Popular works including biographies, commentaries, basic doctrine and Christian living.

MENTOR

Books written at a level suitable for Bible College and seminary students, pastors, and other serious readers. The imprint includes commentaries, doctrinal studies, examination of current issues and church history.

CHRISTIAN HERITAGE

Books representing some of the best material from the rich heritage of the church.

CF4KIDS

Children's books for quality Bible teaching and for all age groups: Sunday school curriculum, puzzle and activity books; personal and family devotional titles, biographies and inspirational stories – because you are never too young to know Jesus!

Christian Focus Publications Ltd,
Geanies House, Fearn, Ross-shire,
IV20 1TW, Scotland, United Kingdom.
www.christianfocus.com